easy food for kids

easy food for kids

simple recipes for child-friendly food

RYLAND
PETERS
& SMALL

LONDON NEW YORK

Senior Designer Sonya Nathoo
Editors Céline Hughes and
Delphine Lawrance
Picture Researcher Emily Westlake
Production Controller
Maria Petalidou
Art Director Leslie Harrington
Publishing Director Alison Starling

Indexer Sandra Shotter

First published in
Great Britain in 2009
by Ryland Peters & Small
20–21 Jockey's Fields
London WC1R 4BW
www.rylandpeters.com

10 9 8 7 6 5 4 3 2 1

Text © Susannah Blake, Tamsin
Burnett-Hall, Linda Collister, Ross
Dobson, Silvana Franco, Liz Franklin,
Tonia George, Nicola Graimes,
Amanda Grant, Rachael Anne Hill,
Louise Pickford, Fran Warde and
Ryland Peters & Small 2009

Design and photographs
© Ryland Peters & Small 2009

ISBN 978 1 84597 897 6

A CIP record for this book is available
from the British Library.

Printed in China

Notes

• All spoon measurements are level,
unless otherwise specified.

• Ovens should be preheated to the
specified temperature. Recipes in this
book were tested using a regular oven.
If using a fan-assisted oven, follow the
manufacturer's instructions for
adjusting temperatures.

• All eggs are medium, unless
otherwise specified. Recipes containing
raw or partially cooked egg, or raw fish
or shellfish, should not be served to
the very young, very old, anyone with
a compromised immune system or
pregnant women.

• The serving amounts given in the
recipes are approximate suggestions
only and will vary depending on
whether they are served to older
children or younger children, or adults.

contents

introduction

It can be all too easy to get stuck in a rut with the children's dinner. When time is precious and the little ones are clamouring for some food, the temptation is to make that fail-safe pasta dish or those favourite chicken nuggets to keep them happy with the minimum fuss. Sometimes all that's needed to bring a little variety and fun back into mealtimes is some simple inspiration. Leaf through this friendly collection of recipes and you'll find something to soothe and delight every hungry tummy.

Do get the kids involved too: if they help you chop vegetables, stir sauces and weigh ingredients (all under supervision of course!), they'll be more excited about the food they are eating, and it will help them learn about ingredients and simple cooking techniques. They can also take pride in the home-made sticky gingerbread in their lunchbox, and the chocolate monkey milkshake they offer when their friends come round after school.

Every meal is covered – breakfast and brunch, lunchboxes, teatime, and dinner, with desserts, drinks, and snacks along the way – so you'll never be lost for dinnertime ideas again.

breakfast & brunch

banana, pecan & granola yoghurt pot

400 g natural bio yoghurt

3 ripe bananas, sliced

50 g pecan nuts

75 g dark brown muscovado or
   dark brown soft sugar

100 g granola

50 g chocolate, grated

makes 4 pots

This balanced breakfast will keep your children's appetites satiated until lunchtime.

Spoon some yoghurt into 4 glasses. Top with the bananas, then add the pecan nuts, brown sugar and granola. Spoon the remaining yoghurt over the top, then sprinkle with the grated chocolate and serve.

frozen berry yoghurt cup

500 g frozen mixed berries

100 g unrefined caster sugar

400 g natural Greek yoghurt

makes 4 cups

During the winter months, summery berries will remind children of days spent playing in the garden. They're also a great source of vitamin C.

Put the frozen berries in a blender with the sugar and blitz into small pieces. Take 4 glasses and fill with alternating layers of yoghurt and berries. Leave for 5 minutes before serving.

muesli

50 g sunflower seeds

50 g pumpkin seeds

25 g linseed (optional)

50 g flaked almonds

50 g hazelnuts, chopped

450 g porridge oats

50 g wheatgerm (optional)

75 g ready-to-eat dried apricots,
   chopped

50 g dried banana

50 g golden sultanas

50 g dried cherries or cranberries

To serve:

1 banana, sliced, or a small handful of
   fresh berries or seedless grapes

cold milk or natural yoghurt

2 baking trays

makes 950 g

The nuts and seeds in this muesli are full of vitamins and minerals while the oats provide slow-releasing energy and the fruit fibre. You couldn't give your kids a better start to the day.

Preheat the oven to 200°C (400°F) Gas 6.

Sprinkle all the seeds and nuts on one baking sheet and the oats on another. Cook in the preheated oven for 10–15 minutes or until lightly toasted then leave to cool.

Once cool, put the nuts, seeds and oats in a large airtight container. Add the wheatgerm (if using) and dried fruit, then close the lid securely and shake well. Store in a cool dry place.

To serve, spoon about 5 tablespoons muesli into a bowl, top with fresh fruit and pour over some milk or add some natural yoghurt.

VARIATION

To make granola, put all the ingredients listed above in a bowl and add 2 tablespoons maple syrup. Mix well. Transfer to a non-stick baking sheet and bake in a preheated oven at 160°C (325°F) Gas 3 for about 40 minutes, stirring halfway through, until crisp and golden. Serve with cold milk.

pink porridge

75 g porridge oats

25 g wheatgerm (optional)

600 ml milk (see Cook's Tip)

75 g raspberries or strawberries, hulled, plus extra for serving

1–2 teaspoons clear honey (optional)

serves 2–4

Oats are an excellent source of slow-releasing sugars, fibre, iron, zinc and B vitamins. The fresh fruit adds a gloriously kid-friendly pink tinge!

Put the oats, wheatgerm, if using, and milk in a large microwaveable bowl and cover with microwaveable clingfilm. Pierce the clingfilm and heat in a microwave on HIGH for 4–5 minutes. Stir and let stand for 2 minutes.

Transfer the porridge to a blender, add the fruit and process until smooth. Add honey, if using, to taste. If necessary, return the porridge to the microwaveable bowl and reheat on HIGH for 1 minute.

To serve, spoon into individual bowls and top with a few whole raspberries or strawberries.

COOK'S TIP

Use whole milk for children under the age of 5, semi-skimmed milk for children over 5.

VARIATION

Replace the strawberries or raspberries with 1 sliced banana and ½ teaspoon ground cinnamon.

scrambled eggs

6 eggs
4 tablespoons milk
2 tablespoons butter
sea salt and freshly ground
   black pepper
freshly chopped chives, to serve

serves 4

Make these scrambled eggs in the microwave or on the hob in a non-stick pan for a creamier, more comforting texture.

Whisk the eggs together with the milk and seasoning. Melt the butter in a medium non-stick pan, then add the egg mixture, stirring frequently until it reaches a creamy consistency. Serve with a sprinkling of chopped chives and hot buttered toast. For a real treat add a few slices of smoked salmon.

poached eggs

4 eggs

serves 2–4

Poached eggs are ready in just five minutes – perfect if you're having to fit supper around a heavy timetable of extra-curricular activities.

Boil a kettle of water and pour into a large saucepan. Crack the eggs into 4 cups, stir the water with a spoon and slip each egg into it. Bring to a gentle simmer, then cover with a lid, remove from the heat and leave to stand: 5 minutes for soft poached eggs, and slightly longer if you prefer the yolk hard. Lift the eggs from the water with a slotted spoon and rest on kitchen paper to remove any excess water. Serve on toast, perhaps with a slice of ham underneath the egg.

scrambled eggs

eggs cocotte

eggs cocotte

60 g fresh spinach, chopped
4 eggs
4 tablespoons milk
75 g Parmesan cheese, grated
sea salt and freshly ground
    black pepper
4 ovenproof ramekins, buttered

makes 4

These iron- and calcium-packed baked eggs go down a treat at breakfast time or as a light meal.

Preheat the oven to 200°C (400°F) Gas 6. Divide the spinach between the prepared ramekins. Crack an egg on top, add a spoonful of milk to each, then season and top with the Parmesan. Place the ramekins on a baking tray in the preheated oven and cook for 6 minutes.

omelette

6 eggs
6 tablespoons milk
50 g butter
sea salt and freshly ground
    black pepper

serves 3

Whether plain or filled with whatever you happen to have in the fridge, omelettes are a great standby meal and a good, inexpensive way of ensuring that your children have enough protein in their diet.

Whisk together the eggs, milk and seasoning. Melt the butter in a large non-stick frying pan, then pour in the egg mixture, using a fork to lift the set egg and let the liquid egg flow underneath. Cook until the top is just soft. Using a palette knife, fold over one-third of the omelette, then turn out and fold over again. Cut into portions and serve at the table.

wholemeal banana
& chocolate muffins

225 g wholemeal flour

2 teaspoons baking powder

100 g unrefined caster sugar

75 g chocolate chips

2 eggs, beaten

100 ml vegetable oil

2 bananas

a 6-hole muffin tin, lined with
*   paper cases*

makes 6 muffins

The chocolate and banana in these muffins make the wholemeal less obvious. Children will gobble them up and get all the benefits of the muffins' high fibre, calcium and potassium content.

Preheat the oven to 180°C (350°F) Gas 4.

Put the flour, baking powder, sugar and chocolate drops in a bowl and mix well. Beat together the eggs and oil and pour into the bowl. Mash the bananas with the back of a fork, add to the bowl and mix together quickly: the mixture will be quite stiff. Take care not to over-mix or the muffins will be heavy. Spoon the mixture into the paper cases and bake in the middle of the preheated oven for 40 minutes. Test for readiness by inserting a knife: the blade should come out clean. Eat warm or cold.

carrot & walnut muffins

130 g unsalted butter or
   polyunsaturated margarine
320 g plain flour (or half and half
   plain and wholemeal flour)
1½ teaspoons mixed spice
1 tablespoon baking powder
150 g light muscovado sugar
230 g carrots, peeled and grated
50 g walnuts, chopped (optional)
2 large eggs, lightly beaten
5–6 tablespoons semi-skimmed milk
12 walnut halves, to decorate

Topping:
90 g low-fat cream cheese
40 g unsalted butter or
   polyunsaturated margarine
40 g icing sugar
½ teaspoon vanilla extract
*a 12-hole muffin tin, lined with
   paper cases*
a wire rack

makes 12 muffins

These muffins are the perfect way to wrap up beta carotene-rich carrots and walnuts that are plentiful in omega-3 fatty acids in kid-friendly packages. Try not to over-mix the muffin mixture as this can give the muffins a heavy texture.

Preheat the oven to 200°C (400°F) Gas 6.

Melt the butter in a small saucepan over gentle heat, then leave to cool slightly.

Meanwhile, sift the flour, mixed spice and baking powder into a large mixing bowl. Stir in the muscovado sugar, carrots and chopped walnuts, if using.

Pour the butter into the flour mixture with the eggs and milk and mix gently with a wooden spoon until combined. Spoon the mixture into the paper cases, then bake in the preheated oven for 20 minutes until risen and golden. Transfer to a wire rack to cool.

To make the topping, beat together the cream cheese, butter, icing sugar and vanilla extract until smooth and creamy. Spread the cream cheese mixture on top of the muffins, then decorate each with a walnut half.

apple & oat muffins

100 g wholemeal self-raising flour

100 g white self-raising flour

2 teaspoons baking powder

1 teaspoon mixed spice

25 g wheatgerm (optional)

50 g light muscovado sugar

50 g sultanas

2 apples, about 225 g, cored and
   finely chopped

25 g pecan nuts, chopped

50 g stoned dates, chopped

120 ml sunflower oil

2 eggs, beaten

2 tablespoons natural yoghurt

1 tablespoon sesame seeds

*a 12-hole muffin tin, lined with
   paper cases*

makes 12 muffins

These muffins are made with sunflower oil and yoghurt, so they are moist without having the high saturated fat content of most commercially-prepared versions. Serve them warm on a cold morning or eat as a snack at any time of the day.

Preheat the oven to 200°C (400°F) Gas 6.

Sift the flours, baking powder and mixed spice into a bowl. Add any bran left in the sieve and the wheatgerm, if using, and mix.

Add the sugar, sultanas, apples, pecan nuts and dates and mix lightly with a wooden spoon. Make a well in the centre, add the oil and eggs and stir to mix. Add the yoghurt and stir lightly, until just mixed (do not over-mix or the muffins will be dry).

Spoon the mixture into the paper cases until three-quarters full. Sprinkle the sesame seeds over the top, then bake in the preheated oven for 15–18 minutes until firm to the touch. Remove from the oven and leave to cool slightly. Serve warm. The muffins can be wrapped and frozen for up to 1 month.

super-healthy blueberry mini-muffins

175 g wholemeal self-raising flour

100 g white self-raising flour

2 teaspoons baking powder

½ teaspoon ground cinnamon

2 ripe bananas

2 eggs

130 g soft brown sugar

90 g polyunsaturated margarine

1 teaspoon vanilla extract

100 g ripe blueberries

a mini-muffin tray, lined with mini-muffin cases

makes 20 mini-muffins

Your little ones will enjoy eating these for breakfast, as a snack or pudding with a dollop of Greek yogurt, ice-cream or crème fraîche. They will also enjoy helping you make them as they really couldn't be simpler. They contain both bananas and antioxidant-packed blueberries. The quantities in this recipe are deliberately quite large as they freeze well.

Preheat the oven to 190°C (375°F) Gas 5.

Sift together the flours, baking powder and cinnamon in a large bowl.

Peel the bananas and put them in a bowl. Mash them with a fork or purée them with a hand-held blender. Add the eggs, sugar, margarine and vanilla extract and blend again. Pour into the flour mix, and mix until just combined.

Gently fold in the blueberries. Spoon into the mini-muffin cases and bake in the preheated oven for 25 minutes, or until risen and golden brown. Turn out onto a wire rack and leave to cool. Store in an airtight container for up to 3 days, or freeze.

blueberry pancakes

a little oil, for greasing

120 g plain flour

a big pinch of salt

1 tablespoon caster sugar

2 large eggs, separated

150 ml milk

25 g unsalted butter, melted

175 g fresh or frozen blueberries

maple syrup, to serve

peanut butter, to serve

makes 12 pancakes

Not only are pancakes cheap and quick to make, they are universally loved by kids. Blueberries add a dose of healthy antioxidants to the batter.

Heat a non-stick frying pan over low heat.

Put the flour, salt and sugar in large bowl and mix well with a wire whisk. Make a well in the centre of the flour and pour in the egg yolks and milk. Using the whisk, mix together the milk and yolks, then stir in the flour gradually. The liquid will become quite thick, and you may need to whisk it more to get rid of the lumps.

Using an electric handheld whisk, whisk the egg whites until they are very stiff. Fold the whites into the other bowl. It is better to have small lumps of white than a completely smooth batter.

Turn up the heat under the pan to medium/low. Add a large spoonful of batter to one side of the pan – it will spread out to about 10 cm across. Drop about 6 blueberries into the centre of the pancake. After about 1 minute, check to see if small bubbles are breaking on the surface of the pancake and it has begun to set. Flip it over to cook the other side. Cook the pancake for another minute, then lift out of the frying pan. Cook the rest of the batter the same way (try cooking 2 or 3 at once). Eat straight from the pan with any leftover blueberries and maple syrup.

buttermilk drop scones
with bananas & maple syrup

250 g plain flour

1 teaspoon bicarbonate of soda

2 teaspoons cream of tartar

1 tablespoon caster sugar

2 eggs

1 teaspoon sunflower oil

300 ml buttermilk

unsalted butter, for frying

slices of banana, to serve

a drizzle of maple syrup, to serve

makes 15–20 scones

Kids will enjoy making these drop scones as much as eating them so get them involved. Don't be afraid to try out different toppings like sliced strawberries and cream or blueberries mixed with Greek yoghurt and honey.

Put the flour, bicarbonate of soda, cream of tartar and sugar in a bowl and make a well in the centre. Add the eggs, oil and half of the buttermilk to the well and gradually incorporate the flour with a whisk. Add the remaining buttermilk and whisk well to make a smooth batter.

Melt a knob of butter in a large, non-stick frying pan. Drop large spoonfuls of batter into the pan from the tip of the spoon to form rounds, spacing well apart. Cook for 2–3 minutes until bubbles appear on the surface and burst, then turn them over and cook for a further 1–2 minutes until golden brown underneath. Put the scones on a clean tea towel and fold it over to keep them warm while you cook the rest of the scones.

Serve the scones warm, topped with slices of banana and a generous drizzle of maple syrup.

cornish bread

300 ml milk

½ teaspoon saffron strands

500 g unbleached white bread flour

1 teaspoon salt

7 g sachet easy-blend dried yeast

150 g unsalted butter, diced, plus extra
   for greasing the loaf tin

50 g light muscovado sugar

100 g mixed dried fruit (sultanas,
   raisins and currants)

a 450-g loaf tin (about 18 x 12 x 7 cm),
   greased with butter and gently
   warmed

makes 1 medium loaf

By making your own bread, you can avoid feeding your children any of the preservatives found in commercially-prepared loaves.

Heat up the milk to hot but not boiling. Pour into a heatproof jug with the saffron, then cover and leave to infuse for 2 to 4 hours.

Put the flour, salt and yeast in a bowl or the bowl of an electric mixer. Mix, then add the butter. Rub it between your fingertips until the mixture looks like breadcrumbs. Mix in the sugar.

Gently warm the milk. Make a well in the centre of the flour mixture, then pour in the milk. Mix until you have a heavy, sticky dough. Knead the dough on a lightly floured work surface for 5 minutes. Mix in the fruit then lift the dough into the warm loaf tin, pressing it down to squeeze out the air bubbles. Put the tin into a large plastic bag and gently inflate the bag to make a tent, so the plastic doesn't touch the dough. Tie the ends closed, then leave in a warm place until the dough has risen to the top of the tin – about 1 hour. Preheat the oven to 180°C (350°F) Gas 4.

Remove the loaf from the plastic and bake for about 1 hour until golden. Turn out onto a rack. If the underside sounds hollow, the loaf is cooked. If not, bake for another 5 minutes. Leave to cool before slicing. Eat within 4 days or freeze for up to 1 month.

soups & snacks

minestrone with pesto

250 g tinned haricot beans
1 tablespoon olive oil
1 red onion, chopped
2 garlic cloves, crushed
2 leeks, diced
2 carrots, diced
2 celery sticks, diced
1.2 litres chicken or vegetable stock
180 g bacon, diced
1½ tablespoons tomato purée
1 bay leaf
a small bunch of thyme
75 g tiny pasta

Pesto:
75 g pine nuts
a generous bunch of fresh basil
75 g Parmesan cheese, grated
2 garlic cloves, crushed
100 ml olive oil

serves 4

This hearty soup will warm up your children's stomachs after a wintry day spent playing with their friends outdoors.

Heat the oil in a saucepan, add the onion, garlic, leeks, carrots, celery and bacon and gently fry for 10 minutes over medium heat without browning. Add the beans, stock, tomato purée and herbs, bring to the boil and simmer for 25 minutes.

Meanwhile, make the pesto. Put all the ingredients in a blender or food processor and whiz until smooth. Transfer to a jar, cover with olive oil and store in the fridge until needed.

When the soup has finished its first simmering, add the pasta and simmer again for 8 minutes, stirring frequently. Season and serve with a spoonful of pesto and lots of crusty bread.

pumpkin soup

1 pumpkin, about 1 kg

1 tablespoon olive oil

1 potato, about 200 g, diced

1 onion, chopped

1–2 garlic cloves, crushed

1 teaspoon ground cumin

900 ml vegetable or chicken stock

1 tablespoon freshly chopped
   sage leaves

150 ml half-fat crème fraîche

To serve, your choice of:

freshly grated nutmeg

finely grated Gruyère or Cheddar
   cheese

roasted pumpkin seeds

croutons

serves 6

This is a really filling, warming soup. Pumpkin is also easy to digest, so it's ideal for kids who are recovering from short bouts of illness.

Cut the pumpkin into small wedges, then scoop out the seeds. Peel and discard the skin then cut the flesh into small pieces.

Heat the oil in a heavy-based saucepan, add the potato, onion and garlic and cook gently, stirring occasionally, for 5–8 minutes until the vegetables are softened but not browned. Sprinkle in the cumin and cook for 1 minute more. Add the stock, pumpkin and sage to the pan. Bring to the boil, reduce the heat, cover and simmer gently for 20–25 minutes until the pumpkin is soft.

Remove the pan from the heat and leave to cool slightly. Transfer the mixture to a blender or food processor and blend, in batches if necessary, to form a smooth purée.

Return the purée to the pan and heat gently. Stir in the crème fraîche, then ladle into warm bowls. Serve sprinkled with freshly grated nutmeg, cheese, roasted pumpkin seeds or croutons.

creamy pea soup

3 tablespoons extra virgin olive oil,
   plus extra to serve
1 small onion, finely chopped
1 garlic clove, crushed
1 small potato (about 100 g),
   finely chopped
700 g peas (fresh or frozen)
1 litre well-flavoured vegetable or
   chicken stock
3 tablespoons double cream
sea salt and freshly ground
   black pepper

serves 4

This creamy, dreamy soup can be made with frozen peas, so it's quick to prepare as well as being packed with vitamins A, C and B9.

Heat the olive oil in a large saucepan, then add the onion, garlic and potato. Cook over gentle heat for 8–10 minutes, stirring regularly, until the onion is translucent and the potatoes are starting to soften.

Pour in the peas and the stock. Leave the soup to simmer for about 20 minutes, until the potato is very soft.

Remove the saucepan from the heat and liquidize the soup with a stick blender until it is smooth. If you don't have a stick blender and are using a food processor or blender, leave the soup to cool a little before you blend it.

Once the soup is smooth, stir in the cream and season to taste with a little sea salt and some freshly ground black pepper. Spoon into warmed soup bowls, garnish with a drizzle of extra virgin olive oil and serve with some good crusty bread.

alphabet soup

100 g cubed smoked pancetta

1 tablespoon olive oil

½ onion, chopped

1 large potato, cubed and rinsed

1 carrot, chopped

2 celery sticks, sliced

2 small courgettes, chopped

3 tomatoes, halved, deseeded and
   chopped

1 litre chicken stock

500 g alfabetto soup pasta

½ small round cabbage, sliced

100 g green beans, cut into 2-cm lengths

100 g peas, fresh or frozen

about 200 g tinned beans, such as
   cannellini, rinsed and drained

salt and freshly ground black pepper

To serve:

2 tablespoons freshly chopped parsley

crusty Italian bread

freshly grated Cheddar cheese

serves 4

This soup is a children's favourite and a sneaky way of getting them to eat their greens. The addition of pulses makes for a filling dish.

Put the pancetta in a stockpot, heat gently and fry until the fat runs. Add the olive oil, heat briefly, then add the onion and cook gently until softened but not browned.

Add the potato, carrot, celery, courgettes, tomatoes and salt and pepper. Add the stock and the pasta and heat until simmering. Cook over low heat for about 15 minutes. Add the cabbage and beans, bring to the boil and cook for 5 minutes, then add the peas and tinned beans and cook for another 2–3 minutes until all the vegetables are tender. Add salt and pepper to taste, sprinkle with parsley, then serve with bread and cheese (shown here melted on top of the bread).

COOK'S TIP

If your children refuse to eat any soups with 'bits' in, cook the pasta and soup separately. Blend the soup element to a purée, then serve in bowls with a big spoonful of the pasta alphabets on top for them to stir in themselves.

sweet & spicy soup

1 onion, finely chopped

2 potatoes, cubed and rinsed

50 g ready-to-eat dried apricots,
   chopped

100 g split red lentils

1 lemon

750 ml vegetable stock

1/4 teaspoon ground cumin

sea salt and freshly ground
   black pepper

1 teaspoon virgin olive oil or a small
   piece of unsalted butter, to finish

serves 4–6

*This family favourite makes a good meal on a
cold day. It is full of wonderful flavours – savoury,
sweet, spicy and aromatic.*

Put the onion, potatoes, apricots and lentils in a large,
heavy-based saucepan. Juice one half of the lemon and add to
the pan. Pour in the stock, then add the cumin, salt and pepper.
Mix well.

Put the pan over medium heat and bring to the boil. Stir, then
cover the pan, turn down the heat and simmer for 30 minutes.
Stir the pan every 10 minutes to stop the lentils sticking.

Remove the saucepan from the heat and liquidize the soup with
a stick blender until it is smooth. If you don't have a stick blender
and are using a food processor or blender, leave the soup to cool
a little before you blend it.

Pour the soup back into the pan. Taste and add more lemon
juice, salt, pepper or cumin as needed. Gently reheat the soup –
be careful, because it can splutter as it comes to the boil. Turn
off the heat and stir in the oil or butter and serve. Leftover soup
will keep in the refrigerator for up to 4 days.

wholemeal breadsticks with avocado & tomato dip

175 g strong wholemeal flour

75 g strong white flour

½ sachet (2 teaspoons) fast action
dried yeast

2 teaspoons light muscovado sugar

1 tablespoon extra virgin olive oil

150–175 ml warm water

Avocado & tomato dip:

1 small ripe avocado

1 small garlic clove (optional)

1 tablespoon natural yoghurt or cream
cheese

1 very ripe tomato, diced

2 large baking trays, lightly greased

makes 10–12 breadsticks

Small children often need snacks to keep them going. These breadsticks contain energy-yielding carbohydrates, making them ideal.

Sift the flours in a large mixing bowl (adding the bran left in the sieve) and stir in the yeast and sugar. Make a well in the centre and pour in the olive oil then gradually add the warm water, mixing the flour into the liquid. Mix to form a smooth dough.

Turn out on a lightly floured surface and knead until the dough feels firm and elastic. Shape into 10–12 balls. Roll on the lightly floured surface into sticks about 8 x 1 cm. Arrange on baking trays spaced well apart. Cover with lightly oiled clingfilm and leave in a warm place for at least 1 hour, or until doubled in size.

Preheat the oven to 230°C (450°F) Gas 8.

Dust the breadsticks with a little white flour and bake in the preheated oven for 12–15 minutes, or until golden brown. Remove from the oven and leave to cool on a wire rack.

To make the avocado and tomato dip, blend all of the ingredients in a food processor until smooth, then eat immediately with the warm breadsticks. The breadsticks will keep in an airtight container for up to 3 days.

cheese straws

50 g wholemeal flour

50 g plain flour

50 g Parmesan cheese, finely grated

75 g mild Cheddar cheese, finely grated

a pinch of cayenne pepper

100 g unsalted butter, cubed

1 egg yolk

1 large baking tray, lightly greased and covered with baking parchment

makes about 20 straws

These cheese straws are rich in calcium, which helps keep bones strong. They are easy to make so get the children involved.

Preheat the oven to 200°C (400°F) Gas 6.

Combine the wholemeal and plain flours, Parmesan, Cheddar and cayenne pepper in a large mixing bowl and rub in the butter until the mixture resembles fine breadcrumbs. Add the egg yolk and mix until the dough comes together.

Roll out the dough on a lightly floured surface until you have a square about 5 mm thick. Cut into long strips or straws and place on the baking tray, leaving a small space between each straw. Bake in the preheated oven for 8–12 minutes, until golden.

Remove from the oven and transfer to a wire rack to cool. Store in an airtight container for 3–4 days. Serve with tomato salsa.

VARIATION

Add a heaped teaspoon of dried mixed herbs to the flour.

puff pinwheels

4 unsmoked bacon rashers
1 tablespoon olive oil
2 spring onions, finely chopped
375 g ready-rolled puff pastry
2–3 tablespoons red pesto
100 g Cheddar cheese, grated

makes 20 pinwheels

Liven up your child's lunchbox with these puff pastry pinwheels instead of a sandwich. Children seem to really like pesto, but if you don't have any in your cupboard, you can try them without.

Preheat the oven to 190°C (375°F) Gas 5.

Cut the bacon into small pieces. Heat the oil in a frying pan and fry the bacon for 5–10 minutes, until cooked. Add the spring onions and cook gently until they are soft. Leave to cool slightly.

Unroll the pastry sheet, spread with the red pesto and scatter over the bacon and spring onions. Top with the grated Cheddar. Carefully roll the pastry, starting with a long side so that you end up with a long, thin sausage shape.

Cut the sausage shape into 20 circles and put onto a baking tray. Bake for 10–12 minutes until risen and golden. Remove from the oven and leave to cool on a wire rack.

sausage & red pepper rolls

plain flour, for dusting

375 g ready-rolled puff pastry

1 tablespoon olive oil

1 onion, finely chopped

1 red pepper, deseeded and finely
    chopped

1 apple, cored and finely chopped

450 g good-quality pork sausagemeat

1 handful fresh parsley, chopped
    (optional)

freshly ground black pepper

1 egg, beaten

2 large baking trays, greased

makes 18–20

Alternative filling:

450 g chicken mince,
    1 tablespoon honey and
    2 teaspoons wholegrain mustard

Sausage rolls are a children's party classic. The red pepper gives them a colourful twist whilst also containing beta-carotene and vitamin C.

Preheat oven to 200°C (400°F) gas 6.

Roll out the pastry onto a dusted work surface until it is approximately 30 cm x 28 cm and then cut in half lengthways.

Heat the oil in a frying pan, add the onion and pepper and fry gently for 5 minutes or until soft. Add the chopped apple and cook for 1 minute. Leave to cool slightly.

Put the sausagemeat into a bowl, add the onion mixture and parsley (if using), season with black pepper and mix together.

Divide the sausagemeat into two and shape each half into a long sausage shape. Place each sausage shape along the long edge of each piece of pastry. Brush the opposite edge of the pastry with beaten egg and roll up from the sausagemeat edge. Seal the pastry edges and turn the rolls over so the seam is underneath.

Cut each roll into 2.5-cm lengths. Cut a small slit in the top of each roll, brush with beaten egg and pop onto the baking trays. Bake for 20–25 minutes. Remove from the oven, transfer to a wire rack and leave to cool.

vegetable mini-frittatas

8 large eggs

125 ml single cream

freshly ground black pepper

2 tablespoons olive oil

4 spring onions, thinly sliced

3 courgettes, chopped into
   1-cm pieces

1 red pepper, deseeded and chopped
   into 1-cm pieces

100 g soft sun-dried tomatoes,
   chopped into 1-cm pieces

125 g Fontina cheese (or Gruyère
   or Swiss cheese), chopped into
   1-cm pieces

a good pinch of dried oregano

*a 12-hole muffin tin, well greased or
   12 flexible muffin moulds*

makes 12 mini-frittatas

These funsize, eggy frittatas are colourful and quick to make. The vegetables can be substituted with what's in season.

Preheat the oven to 180°C (350°F) Gas 4.

Break the eggs into a bowl. Pour in the cream, add some black pepper then gently beat the eggs and cream until combined.

Heat the olive oil in a medium frying pan. Put the spring onions, courgettes, red pepper and a good pinch of oregano into the pan and stir well. Turn up the heat to medium and cook for 5 minutes, stirring regularly, until the vegetables are a light golden brown. Remove the pan from the heat and leave to cool for 5 minutes before stirring in the tomatoes and cheese.

Set the muffin tin on a baking tray. Spoon the vegetable and cheese mixture into the holes, filling each one with an equal amount. Pour the egg mix over the vegetable mixture.

Put the frittatas in the preheated oven to bake for 25 minutes, until puffed, golden and set. Leave to cool for 5 minutes then gently run a round-bladed knife around the inside of each muffin hole. Carefully lift out or tip out onto a serving platter. Serve warm or at room temperature.

cornbread muffins

200 g wholemeal self-raising flour

1 tablespoon baking powder

1/2 teaspoon sea salt

100 g cornmeal

1 teaspoon cumin seeds

1/2–1 red chilli, deseeded and finely
    chopped

2 tablespoons freshly chopped
    coriander

60 g fresh or frozen sweetcorn kernels

300 ml skimmed milk

1 egg, beaten

3 tablespoons sunflower oil

freshly ground black pepper

*a 12-hole non-stick muffin tin, lightly
    greased*

makes 12 muffins

Cornbread is a 'quick' bread that is a favourite
traditional recipe in America. This flavoured
version is made as muffins to serve with a bowlful
of soup or a slow-cooked casserole.

Preheat the oven to 190°C (375°F) Gas 5.

Sift the flour, baking powder and salt into a mixing bowl, tipping
in any bran left in the sieve. Add a grinding of black pepper,
then stir in the cornmeal, cumin seeds, chilli, coriander and
sweetcorn kernels.

Mix the milk, egg and sunflower oil together, then pour onto the
dry ingredients and stir together briefly until just mixed. Spoon
into the prepared muffin tin, then bake in the preheated oven for
20 minutes until risen, firm and lightly browned.

Remove the muffins from the tin and leave to cool slightly on
a wire rack before serving.

lunchboxes

smoked mackerel pâté

smoked mackerel pâté

3 smoked mackerel fillets

125 ml (about 4 heaped tablespoons)
    natural yoghurt

1 garlic clove, roughly chopped

1 tablespoon wholegrain mustard or
    1–2 tablespoons horseradish
    (optional)

freshly squeezed juice of 1 lemon

freshly ground black pepper

fingers of toast or vegetable sticks,
    to serve

makes 4 small tubs

Mackerel has the highest omega-3 content of all oily fish. This pâté makes a good accompaniment to vegetable sticks or use it as a sandwich filler.

Remove the skin from the mackerel fillets and flake the fish into a food processor (or into a bowl if using a stick blender). Add the yoghurt, garlic, mustard and lemon juice and purée until smooth. Season with a little freshly ground black pepper, if liked.

Put the dip into small airtight tubs and store in the fridge, ready to serve. It will keep for 2–3 days.

hoummous

1 x 400-g tin chickpeas, rinsed and
    drained

2 tablespoons tahini (ground sesame
    seed paste)

2 tablespoons freshly squeezed
    lemon juice

2–3 tablespoons olive oil

1 garlic clove, crushed

serves 6–8

This tasty dip contains lots of calcium and protein from the chickpeas and tahini, as well as iron, fibre and magnesium.

Put all the ingredients in a food processor and blend, using the pulse button, to form a smooth purée, about 1 minute. If the mixture is too stiff, add another tablespoon of oil and a little cooled boiled water. Serve with vegetable sticks or breadsticks for dipping. If not using immediately, cover with clingfilm and store in the refrigerator for up to 3 days.

guacamole

2 ripe avocados, peeled, stone
 removed and roughly chopped
2 tablespoons freshly squeezed lemon
 or lime juice
2 ripe tomatoes
1 garlic clove, crushed
freshly ground black pepper

serves 4–6

Avocados have the highest protein content of
any fruit and are a good source of vitamin C.

Put the avocados in a small bowl, add the lemon or lime juice
and toss well. Cut the tomatoes into quarters and remove and
discard the seeds, if you like. Put the tomatoes, garlic, avocado
pieces and black pepper, to taste, in a food processor. Blend for
1–2 minutes until smooth. Transfer to a small serving bowl and
serve with vegetable sticks and breadsticks for dipping.

If not using immediately, cover the bowl tightly with clingfilm
and store in the refrigerator for up to 24 hours.

roasted root dippers

1 sweet potato
1 parsnip
1 carrot
1 potato
2 tablespoons olive oil
a selection of dips, to serve

serves 4–6

This is another great way to encourage your
children to eat more vegetables.

Preheat the oven to 190°C (375°F) Gas 5.

Peel the vegetables and cut them into thick, chunky chips. Put
them in a roasting tin, pour over the oil and toss well to coat. Roast
in the preheated oven for 40–50 minutes, stirring occasionally,
until tender. Serve with dips of your choice.

super-easy sandwiches

It's often tricky to come up with sandwich fillers that are both nutritious and liked by children. Here are a few suggestions. They all make 4.

4 sesame seed bagels, halved

2–3 tablespoons half-fat cream cheese

4 thin slices smoked salmon

5 cm cucumber, sliced

2 tablespoons coleslaw, optional

Smoked salmon bagels: Spread all the bagel halves with the cream cheese. Put a slice of smoked salmon and some cucumber slices on four of the bagel halves. Divide the coleslaw, if using, between them, then top with the bagel lids. Cut each bagel in half. Wrap in clingfilm and store in the fridge until ready to pack.

4 wholemeal pita breads

4 tablespoons hoummous

½ cos lettuce, roughly shredded

8 cm cucumber, thinly sliced

3–4 tomatoes, thinly sliced

1 carrot, grated

25 g half-fat Cheddar cheese, grated

Carrot & hommmous pitas: Warm the pita breads in a toaster or under a hot grill for 1 minute. Leave to cool slightly, then split them. Put 1 tablespoon hoummous in each one. Half fill with lettuce, then add some cucumber and tomato slices and grated carrot. Add some cheese, then wrap in clingfilm and store in the fridge until ready to pack.

1 large avocado, sliced

2 teaspoons fresh lemon juice

1 tomato, thinly sliced

4 wholemeal rolls, halved

2–3 tablespoons low-fat cream cheese

1 Little Gem lettuce, rinsed

100 g thinly sliced roast chicken

Chicken & avocado rolls: Put the avocado slices and lemon juice in a small bowl and mash to a rough purée with a fork. Add the tomato and mix well. Spread each half of the rolls with a little cream cheese. Put a couple of lettuce leaves and 1–2 slices of chicken on top of 4 of the halves. Top with a spoonful of the avocado mixture and put the bread lid on top. Press lightly together, then wrap in clingfilm and store in the fridge until ready to pack.

falafel in pita bread

2 tablespoons olive oil
1 small onion, chopped
1 garlic clove, crushed
2 x 400-g tins chickpeas,
    washed and drained
1 teaspoon ground cumin
1 teaspoon ground coriander
a handful of freshly chopped
    coriander or mint
2 tablespoons mango chutney
freshly ground black pepper
plain flour, lightly seasoned
4–6 pita breads
lettuce, shredded (optional)
1 tomato, sliced (optional)

makes 12 falafel

Falafel is best served in pita, it's easy to eat and tastes great. This is a very quick and simple version of falafel, and is a good way to encourage your children to eat chickpeas.

Heat 1 tablespoon of the olive oil in a frying pan, add the onion and garlic and fry very gently until soft for approximately 5 minutes. Tip the onion and garlic into a bowl, add the chickpeas, cumin and ground coriander, then roughly whiz together with a stick blender.

Add the fresh coriander and mango chutney and season with freshly ground black pepper.

Mould the mixture into 12 balls and flatten into patty shapes. Dip them in the seasoned plain flour so they are lightly coated. Heat the remaining olive oil in the frying pan and fry the falafels on medium heat for 3 minutes on each side until golden brown. Leave to cool, then put into pita breads with the lettuce, tomato and extra mango chutney, if liked.

meaty sandwiches

Leftover roast meat is ideal for lunchboxes as a slice of meat is 1 portion of a child's daily protein requirement. Each of these makes 1 sandwich.

Roast beef with horseradish & cucumber: Spread a tiny amount of horseradish over your chosen bread, top with 2 pieces of roast beef and a few thin slices of cucumber.

Roast pork with apple sauce: Most children love this combo. Split a roll, spread with apple sauce and fill with the pork. The apple sauce adds a wonderful sweetness and helps to bind the pork together.

Roast pork with chutney: If your child likes chutney, mixing it with a cold meat is an easy sandwich filler. Spread some chutney onto your chosen bread and top with 2 slices of pork.

Lamb with mint jelly & baby spinach: Spread some mint jelly onto your chosen bread. Top with 2 slices of lamb and some baby spinach leaves – a great source of iron.

Bacon with watercress & grated carrot: Finely chop 2 grilled bacon rashers and put onto your chosen bread. Top with a handful of watercress and grated carrot.

Grilled bacon with lettuce & tomato: With this combination, it works best if all the ingredients are finely chopped and mixed together, especially for younger children. Put 2 grilled bacon rashers onto some bread. Top with tomato slices and shredded lettuce.

Bacon with egg & tomato: Mash 1 hard-boiled egg, spread onto 2 slices of bread, sprinkle over 2 finely chopped grilled bacon rashers and top with 1 ripe sliced tomato.

sausage & chutney sandwich

1 good-quality sausage
chutney & bread of your choice

makes 1 sandwich

This is a great way of using up leftover sausages from the previous night's bangers and mash.

Thinly slice a cooked cold sausage. Spread some chutney onto your chosen bread and top with the sausage. If your child fancies something more exciting, try the sesame sausages below.

sesame sausages

12 good-quality chipolatas
2 tablespoons runny honey
2 tablespoons sesame seeds
a heavy-based roasting dish

makes 24 sausages

This is a quick recipe idea for sausages – great for lunchboxes, but also a big hit at children's parties. You'll find that adults love these just as much as children do.

Preheat the oven to 200°C (400°F) Gas 6.

Twist the sausages in the middle and then cut in half. Scatter the sausages over the roasting dish and cook in the preheated oven for 15–20 minutes, turning once. Drain off any fat. Add the honey and cook for another 15 minutes, turning a couple of times until the sausages are sticky and golden all over.

Sprinkle the sesame seeds over the sausages and cook for a further 5 minutes.

chorizo & cheese muffins

500 g plain flour

2 teaspoons baking powder

a pinch of salt

freshly ground black pepper

230 g Emmental, Gruyère or
    Appenzeller cheese, cubed

100 g thickly sliced chorizo sausage
    (replace with ham, or sweetcorn
    kernels if you prefer)

2 large eggs

100 g unsalted butter, melted

350 ml whole milk

12-hole muffin tin lined with paper cases

makes 12 muffins

These savoury muffins filled with molten cheese and spicy Spanish sausage make a welcome change to the usual lunchbox sandwich.

Preheat the oven to 200°C (400°F) Gas 6.

Set a large sieve over a mixing bowl. Tip the flour into the sieve, then add the baking powder, salt and a few grinds of pepper and sift these ingredients into the bowl.

Add the cheese to the bowl. Using kitchen scissors, cut up the chorizo into pieces about the same size as the cheese. Add to the bowl and mix well. Make a well in the centre of the mixture.

Beat the eggs with a fork until just broken up. Pour into the well in the mixture along with the melted butter and milk. Mix all the ingredients together with a wooden spoon to make a rough-looking mixture. Spoon equal amounts of the mixture into the prepared paper cases.

Bake the muffins in the preheated oven for 30 minutes, until golden brown. Remove the tin from the oven, leave to cool for a couple of minutes then transfer the muffins to a wire rack and leave to cool completely. Eat warm or at room temperature the same or the next day and store in an airtight container.

leek frittata

3 leeks, cut lengthways then
    finely sliced
100 g pancetta lardons
2 tablespoons olive oil
8 large eggs
a few fresh chives, snipped
sea salt and freshly ground
    black pepper
a crisp, green salad, to serve
*a round ovenproof dish with a diameter
    of about 23 cm*

makes 4–6 slices

Frittatas are similar to omelettes and are eaten all over Italy. You can substitute the leeks for other seasonal vegetables such as courgettes, tomatoes or broad beans and add some grated cheese.

Preheat the oven to 200°C (400°F) Gas 6.

Scatter the leeks over the base of the ovenproof dish along with the pancetta lardons then drizzle with the olive oil.

Roast in the preheated oven for about 15 minutes, until the pancetta is cooked and the leeks are softened.

In the meantime, beat the eggs in a bowl until very smooth. Season with salt and black pepper.

Remove the dish from the oven and carefully pour in the eggs. Scatter over the chives. Bake for another 20 minutes, until the eggs are set.

Serve the frittata hot or cold with a crisp, green salad.

spinach & onion tortilla

5 eggs, beaten

2 tablespoons olive oil

1 large white onion, halved and thinly
   sliced

175 g fresh spinach leaves, washed
   and chopped

40 g Cheddar cheese, grated

sea salt and freshly ground
   black pepper

makes 6–8 slices

Leafy green vegetables like spinach contain omega-3, an important fatty acid known to help concentration. Spinach is also a good source of potassium, calcium and iron. Chop it up and add to omelettes, pasta sauces or fish pies – an excellent way of getting your child to eat greens.

Preheat the grill to high.

Break the eggs into a bowl, season and beat briefly with a fork.

Heat the oil in a large frying pan with a heatproof handle and fry the onion until soft and pale golden. Add the spinach and sauté for a couple of minutes to wilt the leaves.

Pour the egg mixture into the pan, turn the heat down to its lowest setting and cook the tortilla, uncovered, for approximately 8 minutes, until there is only a little runny egg left on the top.

Sprinkle the grated cheese over the top and brown the tortilla under the preheated grill for 1–2 minutes, until the top is golden and bubbling.

Use a palette knife to slide the tortilla out onto a plate. Cut into wedges. Leave to cool and store in the fridge, ready to serve.

chorizo & bean pasties

250 g tinned haricot beans

150 g chorizo, chopped

50 g Manchego or other hard
   cheese, grated

1 tablespoon plain flour

500 g ready-made puff pastry

1 egg, beaten

sea salt and freshly ground
   black pepper

makes 4 pasties

The chorizo sausage adds a lovely spicy zing to these pasties. This recipe is easy to follow so get the kids stuck in too.

Preheat the oven to 180°C (350°F) Gas 4, then lightly oil a baking tray.

Put the haricot beans in a bowl, add the chorizo, cheese and flour, season and mix well. Pour in 50 ml water and stir again.

Roll out the pastry onto a floured work surface to approximately 30 x 30 cm. Cut the pastry into 4 equal squares and spoon the chorizo mixture into the middle of each one. Brush the edges with beaten egg, then fold two opposite corners together to make a triangular shape. Press all round the edges to seal.

Place the pasties on the prepared baking tray and brush the tops with beaten egg. Make a small slash in the top of each pasty, then bake in the middle of the preheated oven for 40 minutes. These savouries can be eaten hot or cold.

chicken & red pepper stew

2 tablespoons olive oil

8 boneless chicken thighs

2 onions, finely chopped

1 garlic clove, crushed

2 red peppers, deseeded and cut into
bite-sized pieces

300 ml chicken or vegetable stock

1 x 400-g tin cannellini beans, drained
and rinsed

freshly ground black pepper

a pinch of light soft brown sugar
(optional)

a heavy-based casserole dish

serves 4

You can make this recipe for an evening meal
and then keep enough for the children's packed
lunch the next day.

Preheat the oven to 180°C (350°F) gas 4.

Heat half the oil in a heavy-based casserole dish, fry the chicken
thighs until lightly browned all over and transfer to a plate. Add
the remaining oil to the casserole dish, then add the onions,
garlic and red pepper and fry gently for 10–15 minutes until very
soft, but not brown. Add the stock to the mixture in the casserole
dish and cook in the oven for 1 hour.

Spoon half of the sauce from the casserole dish into a jug and
whiz with a stick blender until smooth. Put back into the pan.
Add the cannellini beans and chicken to the pan and cook for
another 15 minutes until the chicken is cooked through. Cut the
chicken into bite-sized pieces.

Season with black pepper and a pinch of light soft brown sugar,
if you think it is needed. Serve for dinner and set some aside to
cool for your child's lunch the next day. Wait until it has fully
cooled, put in an airtight container and store in the fridge.

tuna pasta salad

60 g small pasta shapes

2 tablespoons stoned black or green
olives or 2 tablespoons cooked
sweetcorn

5 cm cucumber, chopped

5 cherry tomatoes, halved

200 g tinned tuna

a few fresh chives

Olive oil dressing:

2 tablespoons olive oil

1 tablespoon freshly squeezed
lemon juice

½ teaspoon Dijon or mild mustard

a pinch of salt

a pinch of freshly ground black pepper

serves 2

'Bow-tie' (farfalle) pasta works best in this recipe and will entice the children. You could use cooked sweetcorn instead of olives if the children don't like strong flavours.

Fill a medium saucepan two-thirds full with cold water, then bring to the boil. Add the pasta, stir gently, then let boil until tender – about 8 minutes.

Strain the pasta, then rinse it under the cold tap, so it cools quickly and the starch is rinsed off. Drain thoroughly.

Put the olives, cucumber and tomatoes and tuna in a bowl. Using kitchen scissors, snip the chives into small pieces and add to the bowl.

To make the olive oil dressing, put all the ingredients into a screw-topped jar, and screw on the lid. Shake well, then open the jar and taste the dressing – you may want to add a little more salt or pepper.

Pour the dressing over the salad, then mix everything very gently with a metal spoon. Cover tightly and store in the refrigerator for up to 48 hours.

creamy potato salad

450 g new potatoes, halved
2 tablespoons mayonnaise
1 tablespoon natural yoghurt
a small handful of fresh mint or
    parsley, chopped
1–2 spring onions, finely chopped
2 handfuls of cubed cheese or
    chopped ham if preferred
freshly ground black pepper

serves 4

If you prefer, you can make this salad with white cannellini beans instead of potatoes for added vitamins and protein.

Bring a small pan of water to the boil, add the potatoes and boil for 10–12 minutes until just cooked. Drain.

Mix together the mayonnaise, yoghurt and herbs in a bowl. Season with a little black pepper. Add the potatoes, spring onions and cheese. Mix everything together, leave to cool and store in the fridge until needed.

potato, pesto & tuna salad

450 g new potatoes, halved
2 large handfuls of green beans
    (about 150–175 g)
2 tablespoons green pesto
1 tablespoon olive oil
175 g tinned tuna in sunflower oil,
    drained
a handful of cherry tomatoes, halved

serves 4

Tinned tuna contains omega-3 fatty acids – great for keeping children's concentration levels up.

Bring a small pan of water to the boil, add the potatoes and boil for 10–12 minutes until just cooked. Trim the beans, cut in half and add to the potatoes 2 minutes before the end of cooking time. Drain.

Mix together the pesto and olive oil in a large bowl, add the potatoes and beans, tuna and tomatoes. Mix everything together, leave to cool and store in the fridge until needed.

potato, pesto & tuna salad

oven-roasted vegetables
with chickpeas & couscous

2 tablespoons olive oil

2 garlic cloves, chopped

1 teaspoon sweet paprika

2 red onions, cut into wedges

1 large red pepper, deseeded and
   sliced

1 small butternut squash, unpeeled,
   cut into wedges

200 g cherry or baby plum tomatoes

100 g green beans, trimmed

2 sprigs of fresh thyme

200 g couscous

1 x 240-g tin chickpeas, drained

finely grated zest and juice of
   1 unwaxed lemon

sea salt and freshly ground
   black pepper

1 large roasting tin, lightly oiled

serves 4

Roasting the vegetables will give them a sweeter taste, making them more child-friendly whilst ensuring they get valuable vitamins in their diet.

Preheat the oven to 200°C (400°F) Gas 6.

Pour the olive oil into a large bowl and add the garlic and paprika. Season well and mix. Place the prepared vegetables in the bowl along with the tomatoes and green beans. Stir until they are well coated with the flavoured oil.

Put the vegetables in the prepared roasting tin with the sprigs of thyme. Cook in the preheated oven for 20 minutes, tossing them regularly to ensure even roasting. Reduce the heat to 180°C (350°F) Gas 4 and roast for a further 20 minutes.

Put the couscous in a large bowl and add 275 ml of hot water, stir well, cover and leave to stand for 5–10 minutes. Meanwhile, put the chickpeas in a saucepan of boiling water and allow them to boil for 2 minutes. Drain and add the chickpeas to the couscous, mixing well to fluff up the couscous. Add the roasted vegetables.

Put 4 tablespoons hot water into the roasting tin and mix well to combine with the vegetable juices. Spoon over the vegetables and couscous. Add the lemon zest and juice, mix, then serve.

coleslaw

1 small head or ½ large white or green
  cabbage
2 carrots, peeled and grated
1 red pepper, deseeded and
  thinly sliced
a large handful of raisins
a large handful of peanuts (optional)
2 tablespoons mayonnaise or
  salad cream
1 tablespoon natural yoghurt
1 tablespoon runny honey
freshly ground black pepper

serves 4

You may need to keep trying this recipe if your child turns his or her nose up the first time.

Cut the cabbage into quarters, cut out the core and then thinly slice the cabbage and put it into a bowl. Add the carrots, pepper, raisins, and peanuts.

In a small bowl, mix together the mayonnaise, yoghurt and honey and season with a little black pepper. Add to the coleslaw and mix well. Store in the fridge, ready to serve.

NUTRITION TIP

If your child does not like eating cooked cabbage, making coleslaw is a good way of sneaking it into his or her diet.

lemon shortbread with berries

175 g butter, softened

75 g golden caster sugar, plus extra
    to dust

grated zest of 1 unwaxed lemon

200 g plain flour

50 g cornflour

fresh seasonal fruit, to serve

*a 20-cm square tin, greased and
    base-lined*

makes 10–12 fingers

A finger of home-made shortbread with some fresh berries is an ideal pudding for a summer lunchbox. If your children prefer orange, try adding the zest from one orange instead.

Preheat the oven to 190°C (375°F) Gas 5.

Beat the butter and sugar together until soft, pale and fluffy.

Add the lemon zest, plain flour and cornflour and mix again until it comes together.

Cover the bowl and chill the mixture for 10 minutes, if you have the time. If not, you can cook it straightaway – it will not make a big difference either way.

Press the dough into the prepared tin and bake in the preheated oven for 15 minutes.

Remove from the oven and dust with sugar, if liked. Score the dough into about 12 fingers (score in half and then score each half into about 6 fingers) and leave to cool completely in the tin.

Once cool, cut into fingers and remove from the tin. Store in an airtight container.

date & seed bars

175 g dried dates, chopped

125 g porridge oats

3 tablespoons sunflower seeds
(ground in a spice grinder or
food processor)

125 g wholemeal flour

100 g light muscovado sugar

1 teaspoon baking powder

50 g hazelnuts, very finely chopped

125 g unsalted butter, softened

a 28 x 18-cm baking tin, greased

makes 10–12 bars

Children's tummies are small so it can be hard for them to get all the calories they need in just three main meals per day. These healthy bakes will help boost their calorie intake without all the saturated fats, refined sugars and additives often found in commercially prepared alternatives.

Preheat the oven to 180°C (350°F) Gas 4.

Put the dates and 200 ml water in a saucepan and bring to the boil. Reduce the heat and simmer gently for 20–25 minutes, or until the dates are tender and most of the liquid has been absorbed. Blend in a food processor until smooth. Set aside.

Put the porridge oats, sunflower seeds, flour, sugar, baking powder and hazelnuts in a bowl and mix well. Add the butter and mix in with your fingertips until well combined.

Put three-quarters of the mixture into the prepared baking tin and press down to make a smooth, even layer. Spread the date mixture evenly over the top. Sprinkle over the remaining oat mixture and press down lightly. Bake in the preheated oven for 20–25 minutes. Leave to cool in the tin, then cut into bars and serve. Store in an airtight container for 3–4 days.

cereal bars

100 ml sunflower oil

30 g light soft brown sugar

150 ml golden syrup

250 g rolled oats

100 g mixture of seeds (e.g. sunflower seeds, pumpkin seeds)

60 g dried fruits (e.g. raisins, cranberries or chopped apricots)

a 20-cm square tin, greased

makes 16 bars

These cereal bars contain far fewer additives and sugar than shop-bought ones.

Preheat the oven to 180°C (350°F) gas 4.

Put the oil, sugar and syrup into a pan and heat very gently to dissolve the sugar. Add the rest of the ingredients and mix well. Tip into the tin and bake for 15–18 minutes until set and golden.

Leave to cool for 10 minutes, and then score into 16 bars. Leave to cool completely in the tin, turn out and cut along the marks into 16 bars. Store in an airtight container.

apricot slices

225 g dried apricots

approximately 6 tablespoons orange juice – you may need to add a little more during cooking

175 ml sunflower oil

4 tablespoons runny honey

175 g rolled oats

175 g plain flour (or a mixture of wholemeal and plain flour)

a 20-cm square tin, greased and base-lined

makes 16 bars

Dried fruit is not only naturally sweet but a great source of fibre to keep children healthy.

Preheat the oven to 180°C (350°F) gas 4. Put the apricots and orange juice in a saucepan. Simmer gently for about 15 minutes until the apricots have absorbed the juice.

Gently heat the oil and honey in a pan until the honey dissolves. Add the oats and flour and mix. Put half the mixture in the tin, then cover with apricots and top off with the remaining oat mix. Bake for 20–25 minutes until golden. Score into 16 slices while still warm then cut once cool. Store in an airtight container.

hot dishes

pasta with ham & peas

300 g pasta, such as
    fusilli
1 tablespoon olive oil
1 shallot, diced
1 garlic clove, crushed
200 g cooked ham, chopped
200 g peas, fresh or frozen
    (no need to thaw)
100 ml double cream
2 egg yolks
75 g Parmesan cheese, grated
sea salt and freshly ground
    black pepper

serves 4

This eye-catching dish is rich in flavour but low on ingredients. It's ready in just ten minutes. Get the children to join in with the cooking.

Bring a large pan of salted water to the boil, add the pasta and cook according to the instructions on the packet until it is al dente. Drain and return it to the pan.

Meanwhile, heat the oil in a saucepan, add the shallot and garlic and sauté over low heat until soft.

Put the ham, peas and cream in another pan and heat to a gentle simmer. Take off the heat and add the egg yolks, Parmesan and seasoning. Mix well so that the egg does not scramble. Finally, add the garlic and shallot, toss through the pasta and serve.

zingy pasta

grated zest and freshly squeezed juice
of 1 unwaxed lemon
4 tablespoons single cream
15 g unsalted butter, at room
temperature
75 g watercress sprigs, rinsed
3 big pinches of salt
freshly ground black pepper
250 g thin pasta, such
as spaghetti
75 g freshly grated Parmesan cheese,
to serve

serves 4

A simple pasta dish that's ready in minutes, yet
bursting with flavour. Serve on its own or with
cooked chicken for extra protein.

Fill a large saucepan with water, add a pinch of salt, and set it
over the heat to boil.

Combine the lemon zest and juice, cream, butter, watercress
sprigs and remaining salt in a bowl, then add some black pepper.

Once the water has reached a rolling boil, add the pasta and cook
according to the instructions on the packet, until al dente. Drain
and add to the bowl containing the zingy sauce. The heat of the
pasta will warm the ingredients through and wilt the watercress.

Toss the pasta several times to coat it in the sauce. Eat
immediately, sprinkled with Parmesan.

butterfly pasta with courgettes, sultanas & pine nuts

2 tablespoons sultanas

3 courgettes, thinly sliced

2 garlic cloves, crushed

3 tablespoons olive oil

3 tablespoons pine nuts

grated zest of 1 unwaxed lemon

400 g farfalle pasta

75 g freshly grated Parmesan cheese,
   to serve (optional)

sea salt and freshly ground
   black pepper

serves 4

This is a family favourite. Children love the butterfly shapes but you can substitute them for any short pasta shape that you have to hand.

Put the sultanas in a bowl and cover them with hot water. Leave for about 15 minutes, until the sultanas are nice and plump.

Heat the oil in a large saucepan and fry the courgettes over medium heat for 6–8 minutes, until they are golden. Add the pine nuts and cook for a further 2–3 minutes, until the pine nuts are golden. Add the garlic and cook for just 2 minutes; you don't want it to cook so much that it browns, as it will become bitter.

Drain the sultanas and stir them into the mixture together with the lemon zest. Season the mixture to taste with some sea salt and freshly ground black pepper.

In the meantime, cook the pasta according to the instructions on the packet, until it is al dente. Drain the pasta and toss with the courgette mixture. Serve at once with Parmesan cheese scattered over it, if desired.

smoked trout & farfalle pasta

200 g farfalle pasta

150 g naturally smoked trout fillet
(or fresh salmon if unavailable),
skinned

125 g frozen peas

150 ml single cream

125 g Gruyère cheese, grated

a collapsible steamer

serves 2

This modern twist on traditional carbonara uses smoked trout, which contains healthy omega-3 fatty acids. The dish is ready in just 15 minutes — perfect for when the children are desperate for their dinner and you've had a busy day.

Cook the farfalle according to the instructions on the packet, until al dente. Whilst the pasta is cooking, put a collapsible steamer on top of the pan and steam the trout for 8–10 minutes.

Remove the trout, flake it with a fork and set aside. About 3 minutes before the pasta is done, add the peas to the pan containing the pasta water.

Meanwhile, put the cream and Gruyère in a saucepan and cook over low heat until the cheese has melted.

Drain the pasta and peas and toss with the trout and cheese sauce. Serve in warmed bowls.

niçoise pasta lunchbox

60 g wholemeal pasta spirals or shells
125 g green beans, cut into thirds
1 egg
50 g black olives
200 g tinned tuna, drained and flaked
100 g cherry tomatoes, halved
2 Little Gem lettuces, leaves separated

Dressing:
1 tablespoon freshly squeezed lemon
    juice
1 tablespoon extra virgin olive oil
1 small garlic clove, crushed
2 heaped tablespoons freshly
    chopped fresh basil
sea salt and freshly ground
    black pepper

serves 2

This lunchbox salad is bursting with colour and virtuous ingredients. The wholemeal pasta contains slow-releasing energy that will keep the children going until suppertime.

Cook the pasta in a saucepan of lightly salted boiling water for about 12 minutes or until al dente. Add the green beans to the pan for the last 3 minutes of cooking time. Drain the pasta and beans, then refresh briefly with cold water.

Meanwhile, add the egg to a small saucepan of cold water. Bring to the boil, then simmer for 6 minutes. Drain and rinse under cold water until cool. Peel the egg and cut in half.

Whisk the dressing ingredients together with the seasoning in a mixing bowl. Mix in the pasta and beans, olives, flaked tuna and cherry tomatoes. Divide the lettuce leaves between 2 bowls and top with the pasta and egg halves.

pancetta & chicken meatballs

500 g chicken mince

50 g thinly sliced pancetta, coarsely chopped

6 spring onions, finely chopped

4 garlic cloves, finely chopped

2 red chillies, deseeded and finely chopped

4 tablespoons freshly grated Parmesan cheese, plus extra to serve

1 tablespoon fresh thyme leaves

1 tablespoon olive oil

200 ml red wine

800 g tinned plum tomatoes

a pinch of sugar

300 g pasta, such as conchiglie

sea salt and freshly ground black pepper

serves 4

This perennial children's favourite is made with chicken, bacon and herbs, making it lighter than the traditional all-meat version.

Put the chicken mince, pancetta, spring onions, garlic, chillies, Parmesan and thyme into a bowl. Add plenty of salt and pepper and mix well. Using your hands, shape into 24 small, firm balls.

Heat the oil in a large saucepan, add the meatballs and cook for about 5 minutes, turning them frequently until browned all over. Add the wine and simmer vigorously for 1–2 minutes.

Add the tomatoes, breaking them up with a wooden spoon. Stir in the sugar, then add salt and pepper to taste. Bring to the boil, then simmer very gently, uncovered, for 30 minutes until the sauce is rich and thick.

Meanwhile, bring a large saucepan of water to the boil. Add a good pinch of salt, then cook the pasta according to the timings on the packet, until al dente.

Drain the pasta and return it to the warm pan. Add the meatballs and sauce to the pasta, toss well to mix, then divide between 4 bowls. Serve topped with extra Parmesan.

parsley & pancetta cannelloni

600 ml tomato passata

150 ml red wine

1 teaspoon brown sugar

1 garlic clove, crushed

1 bay leaf

1 tablespoon olive oil

12 dried cannelloni tubes

Parsley & pancetta filling:

1 tablespoon olive oil

1 onion, finely chopped

2 garlic cloves, finely chopped

125 g cubed pancetta

4 tablespoons freshly chopped
  flat leaf parsley

200 g fresh white breadcrumbs

150 ml double cream

grated zest and juice of 1
  unwaxed lemon

150 g mozzarella cheese,
  drained and cubed

sea salt and freshly ground
  black pepper

a baking dish, about 30 x 20 cm

serves 4

These cannelloni are bursting with a wonderful mixture of flavours. This dish reheats well so you can always make extra for the following day.

Preheat the oven to 190°C (375°F) Gas 5.

Put the passata, wine, sugar, garlic, bay leaf and olive oil into a saucepan. Add salt and pepper to taste and bring to the boil. Cover with a lid and simmer for 15 minutes.

To make the filling, heat the oil in a saucepan, add the onion, garlic and pancetta and cook for 4–5 minutes until softened and golden. Add the parsley, breadcrumbs, cream, lemon zest and juice and salt and pepper to taste.

Spoon the filling into the cannelloni tubes and arrange the stuffed tubes in the baking dish. Pour the tomato sauce over the top and sprinkle with the mozzarella. Bake in the preheated oven for 40 minutes, or until the top is bubbling and golden and the pasta is cooked through.

pappardelle with breaded chicken & garlic butter

1 egg, beaten

75 g fresh white breadcrumbs

3 skinless chicken breasts

4 tablespoons plain flour

3–4 tablespoons extra virgin olive oil

300 g pappardelle pasta

75 g butter

2 garlic cloves, crushed

a small handful of fresh flat leaf
  parsley, chopped

25 g Parmesan cheese shavings

sea salt and freshly ground
  black pepper

a large freezer bag

serves 4

Children will go mad for the winning pairing of breaded chicken and thick strands of ribbon-like pappardelle. Turkey or cod work just as well.

Put a large saucepan of salted water on to boil for the pasta. Prepare one bowl with the beaten egg and another with the breadcrumbs. Put one chicken breast in the freezer bag and bash with a rolling pin until flattened out. Spoon some of the flour into the bag, season well and shake until the chicken is coated. Dip the chicken in the egg, then in the breadcrumbs and set aside. Repeat the entire process with the remaining chicken breasts.

Heat the oil in a large frying pan over medium heat and add the chicken in a single layer. Cook for 2–3 minutes, then turn over and cook the other side for the same amount of time, or until golden. When the salted water in the large pan is boiling, add the pasta and cook until al dente. Lift the chicken onto a chopping board. Add the butter to the pan along with the garlic and parsley and cook over low heat until the garlic and butter are about to colour. Season, cut the chicken into strips and return to the pan.

Drain the pappardelle (reserving a cup of the water), then put back in the pan along with the chicken and its juices. Stir well and add the reserved cup of water. Serve topped with Parmesan.

simple vegetable quiche

1 shop-bought wholemeal pastry case

Filling:
100 g broccoli, divided into small
    florets
1 tablespoon olive oil
1 onion, finely chopped
1 small red pepper, sliced into rings
    and deseeded
1 carrot, about 75 g, grated
3 eggs
150 ml semi-skimmed milk (use whole
    milk for children under 5)
1/4 teaspoon freshly grated nutmeg
freshly ground black pepper

To serve (optional):
salad leaves
boiled new potatoes

serves 6–8

Kids love quiche and this meat-free version is a great way of increasing your child's vegetable intake. Almost any type of vegetable can be used, so be creative. The eggs provide an excellent source of protein, zinc, omega-3 fatty acids and vitamins A, D, E and B12.

Preheat the oven to 200°C (400°F) Gas 6. Unwrap the pastry case and put it on a baking tray.

Steam the broccoli florets over a saucepan of gently simmering water for 3 minutes. Plunge them into cold water and drain well.

Heat the oil in a non-stick frying pan, add the onion and fry gently for 5 minutes, stirring frequently. Transfer the onion to the pastry case, spreading it evenly over the base. Arrange the broccoli, pepper and carrot on top of the onion. Put the eggs, milk, nutmeg and black pepper in a bowl and beat well. Pour the mixture over the vegetables in the pastry case.

Bake in the preheated oven for 15 minutes. Reduce the temperature to 180°C (350°F) Gas 4 and continue to bake for about 20 minutes until the filling is set. Serve with salad and boiled new potatoes, if liked.

tomato, basil & mozzarella pizza

Pizza dough:

450 g plain flour

14 g quick yeast

a pinch of salt

a pinch of sugar

225 ml warm water

2 tablespoons olive oil

Topping:

4 tablespoons olive oil

1 small onion, finely diced

2 garlic cloves, crushed

300 ml tomato passata

a pinch of dried oregano

200 g cherry tomatoes

2 mozzarella balls, sliced

a large bunch of fresh basil

sea salt and freshly ground
　　black pepper

2 baking trays or pizza stones

serves 2–4

Younger family members never seem to tire of pizza, so get them involved in the making as well as the eating.

Put the flour, yeast, salt and sugar in a bowl, make a well in the centre, then add the water and oil and gradually draw in the flour to make a smooth dough. Knead for 12 minutes on a lightly floured work surface. Return the dough to the bowl, drizzle with a little oil, then cover and leave in a warm place until doubled in size. This will take 1–2 hours, depending on the temperature.

To make the topping, heat half the oil in a medium saucepan, add the onion and garlic and sauté over medium heat for 6 minutes. Add the passata, oregano and the remaining oil, season and bring to a simmer. Cook for 25 minutes, stirring frequently.

Preheat the oven to 190°C (375°F) Gas 5. Knock the air out of the dough and knead for 5 minutes. Cut in half, roll each piece into a ball and leave to rest for 10 minutes. Lightly flour a work surface and flatten each piece of dough into a circle about 25 cm in diameter. Place each on a baking tray and spread the tomato mixture on top, followed by the cherry tomatoes and mozzarella. Season and drizzle with a little extra olive oil. Put in the oven and bake for 12–15 minutes. Scatter with torn basil leaves, then serve.

charred vegetable pizza

1 courgette, thickly sliced

1 small aubergine, cubed

4 plum tomatoes, halved

8 unpeeled garlic cloves

1 red onion, cut into wedges

a few sprigs of thyme

2 tablespoons olive oil

1 quantity Pizza Dough (see page 116)

150 g dolcelatte cheese, diced

sea salt and freshly ground
    black pepper

a handful of fresh basil leaves,
    to serve

2 baking trays or pizza stones

serves 2–4

Children won't be able to resist this rainbow of vegetables, coupled with oozing cheese. You can always substitute the dolcelatte for mozzarella if your children don't get on well with blue cheese.

Preheat the oven to 220°C (425°F) Gas 7.

Put the courgette, aubergine, tomatoes, garlic, red onion and thyme in a roasting tin. Add salt and pepper and drizzle with the oil. Cook for 30 minutes, stirring from time to time, until softened and a little charred.

Lower the oven temperature to 200°C (400°F) Gas 6. Knock the air out of the dough and knead for 5 minutes. Cut in half, roll each piece into a ball and leave to rest for 10 minutes. Lightly flour a work surface and flatten each piece of dough into a circle about 25 cm in diameter. Spoon the vegetables over the top.

Put in the preheated oven and bake for 10–12 minutes. Remove from the oven and top with the dolcelatte. Return the pizza to the oven and cook for a further 5–10 minutes, until crisp and golden.

Sprinkle with the basil leaves, cut into wedges and serve hot.

fiorentina pizza

350 g young spinach leaves

1 tablespoon butter

2 garlic cloves, crushed

1 quantity Pizza Dough (see page 116)

1–2 tablespoons olive oil

300 ml tomato passata

150 g mozzarella cheese, drained
and thinly sliced

4 small eggs

50 g fontina or Gruyère cheese,
finely grated

sea salt and freshly ground
black pepper

2 baking trays or pizza stones

serves 4

Spinach and egg is a winning combination on a pizza – it's also a great way of making sure your children get some iron and protein in their diet.

Preheat the oven to 220°C (425°F) Gas 7.

Wash the spinach thoroughly and put into a large saucepan. Cover with a lid and cook for 2–3 minutes, until the spinach wilts. Drain well and, when the spinach is cool enough to handle, squeeze out any excess water with your hands. Melt the butter in a pan and cook the garlic for 1 minute. Add the drained spinach and cook for a further 3–4 minutes. Season.

Knock the air out of the dough and knead for 5 minutes. Cut in half, roll each piece into a ball and leave to rest for 10 minutes. Lightly flour a work surface and flatten each piece of dough into a circle about 25 cm in diameter. Brush with a little oil and spoon over the passata. Put the spinach on the bases, leaving a space in the middle for the egg. Put the mozzarella on top of the spinach, drizzle with a little more oil and season.

Put in the oven and bake for 10 minutes. Crack an egg into the middle of each pizza, top with the cheese and bake for another 5–10 minutes, until the base is crisp and the eggs have just set. Serve immediately.

herby trout parcels

8 sheets filo pastry

a little extra virgin olive oil, to brush

4 skinless and boneless trout fillets

1 spring onion, freshly chopped

1 teaspoon chopped fresh coriander

To serve:

boiled new potatoes

sugar snap peas

makes 4 parcels

This dish is a great way of getting kids to eat oily fish. Besides, it's good from time to time to expand their horizons and offer them something a little different from what they usually eat. You can use salmon instead of trout if you like.

Preheat the oven to 190°C (375°F) Gas 5.

Brush two sheets of filo pastry on both sides with olive oil and place them carefully one on top of the other. Repeat with the remaining sheets.

Put a trout fillet on top of a pair of filo sheets, and sprinkle over a quarter of the spring onion and coriander. Roughly roll up the trout, then fold the filo pastry over the trout to make a triangular parcel. Put the parcel seam-side down on a baking tray and bake for 20–25 minutes until cooked through.

Remove the parcels from the oven and leave to cool slightly before serving with boiled new potatoes and sugar snap peas.

upside-down cheese & tomato tart

½ slice of stale white bread

150 g Provolone cheese, thinly sliced

400 g cherry tomatoes

2 tablespoons olive oil, plus extra
   to grease

plain flour, to sprinkle

300 g ready-made puff pastry,

sea salt and freshly ground
   black pepper

a crisp, green salad, to serve

a 23-cm loose-bottomed tart tin

makes 4–6 slices

This attractive tart requires only a few ingredients and is ready to eat in just 30 minutes. The kids will find it fun to make too.

Preheat the oven to 200°C (400°F) Gas 6.

Lightly grease the base of the tart tin. Whiz the bread in a food processor until you get crumbs. Scatter over the the tart tin base. Arrange the cheese slices on top of the breadcrumbs. Scatter with the cherry tomatoes then drizzle with the olive oil and season with salt and black pepper.

Roll out the puff pastry into a circle on a lightly floured work surface. Its diameter should be slightly larger than the tart tin. Lay the pastry over the tomatoes and tuck the edges into the tin.

Bake in the preheated oven for about 25 minutes, until the pastry is golden brown and risen.

Remove the tart from the oven and leave it to cool for about 5 minutes.

Place an upturned dinner plate (larger than the tart tin) over the tin. Carefully flip everything over so that the plate is on the bottom. Pull the tin away and the tart should slip out onto the plate. Serve sliced, with a crisp, green salad.

mini-meatballs & couscous with five-veg sauce

125 g lean beef mince

½ onion, finely chopped

30 g mushrooms, finely chopped

1 garlic clove, crushed

15 g fresh white breadcrumbs

1 teaspoon freshly chopped parsley

2 teaspoons vegetable oil

1 egg yolk, beaten

1 tablespoon extra virgin olive oil

350 g couscous

700 ml hot chicken or vegetable stock

sea salt and black pepper

Five-veg sauce:

2 tablespoons extra virgin olive oil

1 small onion, peeled and chopped

1 garlic clove, crushed

2 carrots, chopped

1 small courgette, chopped

75 g mushrooms, sliced

1 x 400-g tin chopped tomatoes

125 ml vegetable stock

1 teaspoon dried oregano

½ teaspoon brown sugar

serves 2–4

Not only is this ingenious little recipe quick and easy to make, it's packed with vegetables and children simply can't get enough of it.

Preheat the oven to 180°C (350°F) Gas 4.

Mix the beef, onion, mushrooms, garlic, breadcrumbs, parsley, vegetable oil, egg yolk and seasoning in a bowl. Shape into 12 mini-meatballs. Refrigerate while you make the sauce.

To make the five-veg sauce, heat the olive oil in a saucepan, add the onion and garlic, and sauté for about 3 minutes. Add the carrots, courgette and mushrooms and cook for about 15 minutes, or until softened.

Add the tomatoes, vegetable stock, oregano and brown sugar, season to taste and simmer for 10 minutes. Purée with a stick blender, then leave over low heat to keep warm.

Put the couscous in a large bowl and pour in the hot stock. Cover and leave for 5 minutes. Fluff up the grains with a fork.

Lightly dust the mini-meatballs with flour. Heat the olive oil in a large, non-stick frying pan and cook the mini-meatballs for 8–10 minutes, turning frequently, until cooked through. Serve with the couscous and sauce.

oven-fried chicken nuggets
with potato wedges

100 g fresh breadcrumbs

1 teaspoon sweet paprika

¼ teaspoon dried mixed herbs or
   herbes de Provence

a good pinch of salt

freshly ground black pepper

4 medium chicken breasts, skinless
   and boneless, sliced into strips

50 g unsalted butter, melted

*a large non-stick baking tray or roasting
   tin, lightly oiled*

Potato wedges:

4 baking potatoes, scrubbed and each
   cut into 6 wedges

4 tablespoons olive oil

a non-stick roasting tin

serves 4

Make your very own healthier version of chicken nuggets. Serve with Thai sweet chilli dipping sauce or ketchup, if the children can't resist it.

Preheat the oven to 200°C (400°F) Gas 6.

Put the potato wedges in the roasting tin. Spoon over the oil, and sprinkle with salt and pepper. Toss the wedges so that they are evenly coated in the oil. Put them skin-side down in the tin and bake in the preheated oven for about 1 hour, until brown.

Put the breadcrumbs into a large, clean plastic bag. Add the paprika, dried herbs, salt and pepper. Close the bag and shake well to mix. Dip each strip of chicken into the melted butter then put it into the plastic bag with the crumbs. When all the chicken strips are in the bag, close it tightly and shake it well so the chicken gets coated in the crumbs. Remove each chicken strip from the bag and put it on the prepared baking tray, arranging the strips slightly apart and in one layer.

20 minutes before the potato wedges are ready, put the nuggets in the oven and bake for 15–20 minutes, until golden brown and crisp. Serve the chicken nuggets and potato wedges together.

nut burgers

225 g mixed unsalted nuts, such as
    cashews, walnuts and peanuts
2 tablespoons olive oil
1 onion, very finely chopped
2 garlic cloves, crushed
75 g button mushrooms, finely
    chopped
1 small yellow pepper, deseeded
    and finely chopped
100 g fresh wholemeal breadcrumbs
100 g carrot, grated
1 tablespoon freshly chopped parsley
2–3 fresh sage leaves, finely chopped
1 egg, beaten
wholemeal flour, for coating
sea salt and black pepper

To serve:
4 wholemeal bread rolls
salad leaves
4 tomato slices
tomato ketchup
a baking tray, lightly greased

serves 4–6

Nuts are a good source of fibre, essential fatty acids and protein, making these burgers a healthier option for children than fast food fare.

Put the nuts in a food processor and blend until finely chopped.

Heat 1 tablespoon of the oil in a heavy-based saucepan, add the onion and garlic and fry gently, stirring occasionally, for 5 minutes or until soft and golden. Add the mushrooms and pepper and cook for 3 more minutes. Remove the pan from the heat and mix in all the remaining ingredients except the flour and the remaining oil.

Using your hands, bring the mixture together to form a large ball, adding a little water if the mixture is too dry. Shape the mixture into 4 burgers. Put the flour in a shallow dish and coat the burgers evenly with it. Transfer to a plate, lightly cover with clingfilm and refrigerate for 30 minutes. Preheated the oven to 190°C (375°F) Gas 5.

Put the burgers on the prepared baking tray and brush lightly with the remaining oil. Bake in the preheated oven for 20 minutes until golden and piping hot. To serve, put a burger in a wholemeal bread roll, top with crisp salad leaves, a slice of tomato and a dollop of ketchup.

pan-fried mini-beefcakes
with sautéed spring greens

2 tablespoons vegetable oil

1 small onion, diced

125 g lean beef mince

½ teaspoon dried thyme

200 g potatoes, boiled for 12 minutes,
    then mashed together with 25 g
    unsalted butter

1 tablespoon freshly chopped parsley

1 tablespoon tomato ketchup

a dash of Worcestershire sauce

a little plain flour, to dust

a knob of unsalted butter

6 large spring green leaves, shredded

baked beans, to serve (optional)

sea salt and freshly ground
    black pepper

makes 12 mini-beefcakes

If your children like sausages and meatballs they'll love this. Get them involved in making this simple recipe too. The beefcakes freeze well so make extra for busier days.

Heat 1 tablespoon of the vegetable oil in a saucepan and fry the onion for 3–4 minutes. Add the beef and fry for 3–4 minutes. Stir in the thyme and season. Cook for another minute.

Stir the mixture into the mashed potato with the parsley, tomato ketchup and Worcestershire sauce. Leave to cool, then cover and refrigerate until cold.

Form the mixture into 12 mini-beefcakes, dust with flour, cover and refrigerate for another hour.

Heat the remaining vegetable oil in a large frying pan and sauté the beefcakes for about 5 minutes, or until they are golden and cooked through.

Melt the butter in a large, non-stick frying pan, add the shredded spring greens and sauté for 4–5 minutes, stirring frequently.

Serve the beefcakes and spring greens with baked beans on the side (if using).

lamb koftas with pita pockets

500 g lean lamb mince

1 small red onion

2 teaspoons mild paprika

1½ teaspoons ground coriander

1½ teaspoons ground cumin

¼ teaspoon ground cinnamon

4 grinds of freshly ground black
    pepper

a good pinch of salt

a few sprigs of fresh flat leaf parsley
    or coriander, snipped

Yoghurt dip:

200 ml natural yoghurt

a good pinch of salt

freshly ground black pepper

a small bunch of chives, snipped

a few sprigs of fresh flat leaf parsley
    or coriander, snipped

8 small pitas, to serve

16 wooden skewers

a baking tray or roasting tin, lined with
    foil and oiled

makes 16 koftas

Children love eating with their hands and these tasty koftas are just the thing. In summer, pop them on the barbeque for an outdoor feast.

Preheat the oven to 220°C (425°F) Gas 7. Soak the skewers in a bowl of water to stop the wood from burning in the oven.

Meanwhile, make the kofta mix. Tip the lamb mince into a large mixing bowl. Grate the onion onto the lamb using the coarse side of a grater.

Put the spices, salt and herbs in the bowl and mix. Divide the meat mixture into 16 even portions. Using your hands, mould each portion of meat around a skewer to make an egg or sausage shape about 10 cm in length and place on the prepared baking tray. Cook the koftas in the preheated oven for 15 minutes, until well-browned.

While the meat is cooking, make the yoghurt dip by mixing the yoghurt with the salt and pepper. Mix the herbs into the yoghurt then spoon the dip into a serving bowl.

When the koftas are ready, transfer the skewers to a plate and serve with the yoghurt dip and warm pitas.

fish cakes

500 g white fish fillet such as
 cod loin or haddock
300 ml semi-skimmed milk (use
 whole milk for children under 5)
a handful of fresh flat leaf parsley
1 bay leaf
400 g potatoes, cut into large chunks,
 boiled for 12 minutes then mashed
1 tablespoon finely grated unwaxed
 lemon zest
2 tablespoons freshly chopped herbs,
 such as dill, parsley or coriander
2–3 tablespoons wholemeal flour
2–3 tablespoons sunflower oil
sea salt and freshly ground
 black pepper

Lemony green beans:
150 g green beans
1 tablespoon freshly squeezed
 lemon juice
1 tablespoon extra virgin olive oil

makes 8 small fish cakes

Even children who turn up their noses at fish will usually eat fish cakes. These are packed with quality fish and are completely additive-free.

Rinse the fish and put it in a frying pan with the milk, parsley sprigs and bay leaf. Bring to the boil, then cover and simmer for about 10 minutes until the fish is cooked and the flesh looks white. Remove the fish with a slotted spoon and transfer it to a large bowl. Leave it to cool slightly then remove the skin and any bones and flake the flesh. Discard the cooking liquor.

Add the mashed potato, lemon zest and chopped herbs to the fish. Season to taste with salt and pepper, then mix lightly. Using your hands, shape the mixture into 8 small fish cakes. Put the flour on a plate and coat the fish cakes in it. Transfer the fish cakes to a plate, cover lightly with clingfilm and chill in the refrigerator for at least 30 minutes.

To make the lemony green beans, lightly steam the beans for about 5 minutes. Drain then put in a serving bowl, along with the lemon juice, olive oil and a sprinkling of salt. Toss well and cover.

To cook the fish cakes, heat the oil in a frying pan. Add the fish cakes and cook for 4–5 minutes on each side until crisp and golden brown. Serve immediately with the lemony green beans.

beef bourguignon

1 tablespoon extra virgin olive oil

675 g braising steak, cubed

2 onions, chopped

2 carrots, chopped

1 garlic clove, crushed

1 x 400-g tin chopped tomatoes

300 ml vegetable stock

2 teaspoons freshly chopped herbs
   of your choice

1 tablespoon tomato purée

160 g button mushrooms

a knob of unsalted butter

6 large spring green leaves, shredded

sea salt and freshly ground
   black pepper

mashed potato, to serve

serves 4

The beef and spring greens make this an iron-packed dish. It may sound very sophisticated and grown up but children will love it too.

Preheat the oven to 190°C (375°F) Gas 5.

Heat the oil in a flameproof casserole dish. Add the steak and cook until evenly browned. Remove from the dish and set aside.

Add the onions, carrots and garlic to the casserole and cook until softened. Return the steak to the casserole along with the tomatoes, stock, herbs, tomato purée and some seasoning. Bring to the boil. Cover with a lid and cook in the preheated oven for 1½ hours.

Add the mushrooms and return to the oven, still covered, for a further 30 minutes.

Melt the butter in a large, non-stick frying pan, add the shredded spring greens and sauté for 4–5 minutes, stirring frequently.

Serve the beef bourguignon with the spring greens and mashed potato on the side.

goan prawn curry

1 tablespoon ground coriander

½ tablespoon paprika

1 teaspoon ground cumin

½ teaspoon cayenne or hot chilli powder

½ teaspoon ground turmeric

3 garlic cloves, crushed

2 teaspoons grated fresh ginger

250 g green beans, halved

1 tablespoon tamarind paste or freshly squeezed lemon juice

25 g creamed coconut, grated

400 g uncooked tiger prawns, shelled and deveined

100 g young leaf spinach, rinsed

sea salt and freshly ground black pepper

basmati rice or chapattis, to serve

serves 4

This quick curry will fill your kitchen with a wonderful aroma as it cooks. If your children are a little shy of spicy dishes, simply add less cayenne or hot chilli powder.

Mix the spices to a paste with a little water in a saucepan. Stir in the garlic, ginger and 400 ml cold water, add seasoning and bring to the boil. Simmer for 10 minutes until the sauce has reduced slightly and the raw flavour of the spices is released.

Meanwhile, cook the green beans in a separate saucepan of lightly salted boiling water for about 5 minutes or until tender, then drain and put to one side.

Stir the tamarind paste or lemon juice and creamed coconut into the spicy sauce base until smooth. Add the prawns and cook for about 2 minutes or until they turn pink and are cooked through. Stir in the green beans and spinach and cook briefly until the spinach has wilted. Ladle the curry into bowls and serve with basmati rice or chapattis.

chilli con carne

225 g beef mince

2 tablespoons extra virgin olive oil

1 onion, finely chopped

1 carrot, finely chopped

1 red pepper, deseeded and finely
   chopped

1 garlic clove, crushed

1 tablespoon mixed dried herbs

1 x 400-g tin chopped tomatoes

150 ml beef stock

sea salt and freshly ground
   black pepper

To serve:

white long-grain rice

nachos

guacamole

soured cream

serves 3–4

This dish is effective in boosting iron levels (the mineral most likely to be lacking in children and adults alike) as the vitamin C in the tomatoes increases the body's capacity to absorb iron from the beef mince.

Heat a non-stick frying pan and add half the mince. Dry-fry over high heat to colour the meat. Break up any lumps with the back of a fork. Repeat with the rest of the mince and drain off any fat.

Heat the olive oil in a separate saucepan and cook the onion, carrot and red pepper until they start to soften.

Stir in the garlic and the herbs and cook for 2 minutes. Stir in the tomatoes and the stock and season well. Add the mince and simmer gently for 40–50 minutes until thick.

Serve with rice or nachos and a tablespoon each of guacamole and soured cream per person.

fish pie

500 g potatoes, cut into large chunks,
   boiled for 12 minutes then mashed
500 g cod or haddock fillet, rinsed
400 ml semi-skimmed milk (use
   whole milk for children under 5)
1 bay leaf
250 g tinned mackerel fillets in oil,
   drained and flaked into small
   pieces
2 hard-boiled eggs, roughly chopped
200 g baby spinach leaves, steamed
   and excess water squeezed out
150 g frozen peas, steamed
5 tablespoons sunflower oil
4 tablespoons plain flour
1 large leek, thinly sliced
50 g Cheddar cheese, grated
sea salt and freshly ground
   black pepper
8 ramekins or small ovenproof dishes,
   150 ml each

makes 8 little pies

Protein, essential fatty acids, calcium, iron, fibre – you name it, this fish pie has got it. Every bite will help build fitter, stronger little bodies.

Preheat the oven to 190°C (375°F) Gas 5.

Put the cod, milk and bay leaf in a frying pan and bring to the boil. Reduce the heat and simmer for 10 minutes. Remove from the heat and strain off, reserving the cooking liquor. When the fish is cool, remove the skin and any bones, then flake it. Add the mackerel, along with the chopped eggs, steamed spinach and peas and divide between the 8 ramekins.

Make the reserved cooking liquor up to 400 ml, if necessary, with more milk or water. Heat 4 tablespoons oil in a small pan and stir in the flour. Cook over low heat, stirring continuously, for 2 minutes. Take off the heat and stir in the reserved cooking liquor. Return the pan to the heat and cook, stirring continuously, until the sauce thickens. Season then add to the ramekins.

Heat the remaining oil in a frying pan. Add the leek and cook for 5 minutes until softened. Divide the leeks between the ramekins, then top with the mashed potato. Sprinkle with cheese. Bake in the preheated oven for 20–25 minutes until golden brown and bubbling. Serve immediately.

easy ratatouille & couscous

1 large green pepper, deseeded
  and diced

1 x 400-g tin chopped tomatoes

1 large courgette, diced

1 aubergine, diced

1 onion, thinly sliced

1 carrot, diced

1 celery stick, diced

1 garlic clove, crushed

1 bay leaf

1 tablespoon finely chopped fresh
  basil

400 g freshly cooked couscous

serves 3–4

This ratatouille is packed with vegetables. It makes a versatile sauce and freezes well too – serve it with couscous or with pasta, potatoes or rice. You can also try adding flaked tinned tuna or fresh mackerel to it for extra goodness.

Put the pepper, tomatoes, courgette, aubergine, onion, carrot, celery, garlic and bay leaf in a large saucepan and bring to the boil. Skim off any sediment.

Cover and simmer for about 20 minutes, or until all the vegetables are tender and most of the liquid has evaporated. If there is too much liquid, remove the lid and boil briskly for a few minutes to burn some of it off.

Remove the bay leaf and stir in the basil. Leave to cool slightly, then serve with the couscous.

tarragon chicken casserole

4 skinless and boneless chicken
   thighs, about 335 g, diced
2 large leeks, cut into chunks
2 garlic cloves, crushed
150 ml chicken stock
grated zest and freshly squeezed
   juice of ½ unwaxed lemon
1 tablespoon freshly chopped
   tarragon, or 1 teaspoon dried
   tarragon
1 x 410 g-tin haricot beans, drained
   and rinsed
200 g fine green beans
2 tablespoons crème fraîche
sea salt and freshly ground black
   pepper
a flameproof casserole dish

serves 4

As well as being extremely tasty, this casserole has all the fibre and lean protein needed to keep your children going. The garlic and leeks both contain potent anti-bacterial and anti-viral properties too.

Season the chicken and dry-fry in a non-stick frying pan for 3 minutes until browned. Transfer to the casserole dish. Add the leeks and garlic to the frying pan with 2 tablespoons of the stock and cook for 2 minutes, then tip into the casserole.

Pour the remaining stock into the casserole and add the lemon zest and juice, tarragon and haricot beans. Bring to a simmer, cover and cook gently for 15 minutes.

Stir in the green beans, re-cover and cook for a further 5 minutes until the beans are tender but still have some bite. Finally, spoon in the crème fraîche just before serving.

mozzarella-topped herby vegetable loaf

240 g carrots, grated

1 red onion, finely chopped

2 garlic cloves, crushed

3 celery sticks, finely chopped

125 g mushrooms, sliced

1 small courgette, sliced

1 tablespoon freshly chopped parsley

2 tablespoons freshly chopped
   coriander

60 g Cheddar cheese, grated

2 eggs

125 g wholemeal flour

150 g mozzarella, grated

Sauce:

3 tablespoons extra virgin olive oil

1/2 onion, sliced

1 garlic clove, crushed

2 x 400-g tins chopped tomatoes

1 teaspoon sugar

sea salt and freshly ground
   black pepper

a 450-g loaf tin

serves 3–4

Children can get involved in making this tasty, vegetarian loaf. It's packed with vegetables, ensuring a balanced meal.

Preheat the oven to 180°C (350°F) Gas 4. Line the loaf tin with greaseproof paper.

Mix all the loaf ingredients except the mozzarella in a large bowl. Spoon into the prepared loaf tin and bake for 1 hour.

Meanwhile, to make the sauce, heat the olive oil in a saucepan. Add the onion and garlic, cover with a lid and sweat over gentle heat until soft and pale golden. Add the tinned tomatoes to the onion mixture. Stir in the sugar and season to taste. Cook, uncovered, for about 30 minutes, or until the tomato softens.

Remove the loaf from the oven and leave to stand for 5 minutes. Preheat the grill to hot.

Tip the loaf out onto a plate and slice. Put the slices into a shallow, ovenproof dish. Pour over the tomato sauce and sprinkle with grated mozzarella. Grill for 4–5 minutes, or until the cheese is bubbling and golden. Serve immediately.

salmon skewers

600 g salmon fillet, cut into chunks

freshly squeezed juice of
½ small lemon

a small bunch of fresh chives, snipped

sea salt

450 g cherry tomatoes

3 tablespoons olive oil

lemon wedges, to serve

12 wooden skewers, about 30 cm long

a ridged griddle pan

a pastry brush

makes about 12

These salmon skewers are especially tasty grilled on the barbecue, but you can cook them just as easily on a griddle pan too. Salmon is a great source of healthy omega-3 fatty acids.

Soak the skewers in a dish of cold water for 30 minutes. This will stop them burning when you put them on the hot griddle pan.

Combine the salmon, lemon juice and chives in a large bowl and season with a little salt.

Push a chunk of salmon onto a skewer and then a tomato. Continue threading alternate pieces of salmon and tomato until you have just 6 cm clear at each end of the skewers.

Heat a ridged griddle pan until quite hot. Brush the olive oil over the skewers with a pastry brush. Lay them on the hot griddle pan and cook for about 5–6 minutes, until the salmon is cooked through and golden brown. Turn them over once halfway through cooking. You will need to cook them in batches.

Serve with lemon wedges.

puddings

berry berry peachy purée

berry berry peachy purée

50 g frozen summer berries
1 ripe peach, stoned, peeled
  and chopped
1 fresh mint leaf, chopped
1 tablespoon natural yoghurt
  or fromage frais

serves 1

Berries are packed full of immune-boosting vitamin C and disease-fighting antioxidants. They taste delicious too, especially when mixed with yoghurt or fromage frais.

Put the summer berries, peach and mint in a saucepan and simmer for about 5 minutes, or until the berries have thawed and collapsed a little. Leave to cool slightly, then press through a sieve into a bowl and stir in the yoghurt or fromage frais.

little cherub's cherry semolina

6 sweet cherries, stoned
1 tablespoon pure apple juice
1 ripe banana
1 tablespoon semolina

serves 1

This recipe combines delicious cherries and bananas with semolina to make it a little more substantial – perfect for breakfast or dessert.

Put the cherries and apple juice in a small saucepan and simmer for 2 minutes.

Peel and mash the banana, add it to the pan and simmer for just under 1 minute.

Stir in the semolina and serve, or purée to the desired consistency using a stick blender.

fresh fruit jellies

Orange jelly:

1 packet orange jelly

1 tin mandarins or fresh satsumas

Raspberry jelly:

1 packet raspberry jelly

1 tin raspberries or fresh or frozen
   raspberries

Lemon jelly:

1 packet lemon jelly

1 tin citrus fruits or fresh orange,
   peach or apricots

Strawberry jelly:

1 packet strawberry jelly

fresh or frozen strawberries
   or raspberries

5–6 jelly moulds

serves 5–6

Jelly is something all children enjoy, so why not put some in their lunchbox as a tangy treat? Add some seasonal fresh fruit or tinned fruit to the pots before you pour over the jelly. You can also make the jelly with a mix of fruit juice and water.

If you are using tinned fruit, melt the jelly with the recommended amount of water (usually 100 ml). Then add the juice from the tin of fruit and enough water to make it up to the right volume according to the packet instructions. If using fresh fruit, follow the packet instructions for the jelly.

Mash half the tinned or fresh fruit to a pulp and add to the jelly. Divide the remaining fruits between the jelly moulds. Pour the fruity jelly mixture over the fruit in each mould and leave to set in the refrigerator overnight.

oatmeal pots with warm strawberry sauce

4 tablespoons fine or medium
　　ground oatmeal
200 ml whole milk
½ dessert apple, peeled and cored
4 tablespoons crème fraîche
4 strawberries, hulled and sliced,
　　to decorate

Strawberry sauce:
225 g strawberries
1 tablespoon freshly squeezed
　　lemon juice
about 25 g caster sugar, to taste

serves 2

This tasty dessert is full of berry goodness and will satisfy a sweet tooth without overloading your child with sugar. Adults will love them too.

Put the oatmeal and milk in a small bowl and grate in the apple. Stir, cover and refrigerate for about 8 hours.

To make the strawberry sauce, put the strawberries, 150 ml water, the lemon juice and enough sugar to taste in a heavy-based saucepan. Heat gently, stirring occasionally, until the sugar has dissolved. Bring to the boil, reduce the heat and simmer for 5 minutes, or until the strawberries are really soft.

Purée the stewed strawberries in a blender, then strain through a sieve to get a smooth sauce.

Divide the apple and oatmeal mixture between 2 small bowls with 2 tablespoons crème fraîche and pour over the warm strawberry sauce. Decorate with the sliced strawberries.

iced lollies

600 ml freshly squeezed fruit juice,
    such as orange, apple or pineapple
    juice or 450 g fresh ripe fruit, such
    as strawberries, raspberries or a
    mixture of both
40–50 g unrefined caster sugar
    (optional)
8 iced lolly moulds, 80 ml each

makes 8 lollies

These juicy, tangy lollies are a real summer treat for children and versatile too. They are full of the goodness of fresh fruit.

Set the freezer to rapid freeze. Rinse out the iced lolly moulds with cold water and put them in their rack.

If using fruit juice, carefully pour the juice into the moulds, then push the handle tops into the lollies.

If using fresh ripe fruit, remove any stalks, rinse lightly and cut any large fruit in half. Put the fruit in a saucepan, add sugar to taste and 150 ml water. Cook over gentle heat for 5 minutes or until the fruit has collapsed. Leave to cool slightly, then transfer to a food processor or blender and process to form a purée. Push the purée through a fine, non-metallic sieve to remove the pips.

Make the purée up to 600 ml with water or freshly squeezed orange juice. Pour it into the iced lolly moulds, then push a handle top into each lolly. Freeze for at least 4 hours until frozen. Use within 2–3 days.

knickerbocker glory

knickerbocker glory

500 g raspberries

4 scoops chocolate ice cream

300 ml natural yoghurt

225 g strawberries, halved if large

8 scoops vanilla ice cream

50 g plain chocolate
   (at least 70 percent cocoa solids),
   roughly chopped or grated

4 tall sundae glasses

serves 4

No childhood would be complete without the experience of eating a knickerbocker glory. These are packed full of fruit rich in vitamin C.

Put 1 tablespoon of raspberries in the bottom of each glass and top with 1 scoop of chocolate ice cream. Spoon over one-quarter of the yoghurt in each glass, then top with one-quarter of the strawberries, reserving 4 of the strawberries to decorate.

Add 1 scoop of vanilla ice cream, then scatter over a little chopped chocolate. Add 1 more tablespoon of raspberries to each glass, then finish with 1 scoop of vanilla ice cream. Sprinkle with a little more chopped chocolate, top with a strawberry and serve immediately.

sticky toffee & apricot sauce

175 g ready-to-eat dried apricots,
   roughly chopped

25 g light muscovado sugar

15 g butter

makes 300 ml

This wonderfully sticky sauce makes a fantastic accompaniment to ice cream.

Put the apricots, sugar and 200 ml water in a heavy based saucepan. Bring to the boil, then cover and reduce the heat. Simmer for 12–15 minutes or until the apricots are really soft. Leave to cool slightly, then transfer to a blender and process to form a purée. Return the purée to the rinsed pan, add the butter and heat gently until the butter has melted. Serve over ice cream.

lemon polenta cake

175 g butter, softened

175 g unrefined caster sugar

100 g polenta

½ teaspoon baking powder

175 g ground almonds

grated zest and freshly squeezed
   juice of 1 unwaxed lemon

½ teaspoon vanilla extract

3 eggs

Syrup:

finely grated zest and freshly squeezed
   juice of 2 unwaxed lemons

50 g icing sugar

*a springform cake tin, 24 cm in
   diameter, lightly greased*

serves 6–8

Children will love this sticky, syrupy cake. The polenta and ground almonds give it a wonderfully moreish texture. Serve it for dessert with crème fraîche or for afternoon tea.

Preheat the oven to 180°C (350°F) Gas 4.

Beat together the butter and sugar until creamy. Add the polenta, baking powder, ground almonds, lemon zest and juice, vanilla extract and eggs. Mix together until smooth. Spoon the mixture into the prepared tin and bake in the middle of the preheated oven for 30 minutes.

Meanwhile, make the syrup. Put the lemon zest and juice in a small saucepan with the icing sugar and 2 tablespoons of water. Bring to the boil and simmer for 2 minutes. When the cake is done, let cool slightly in the tin, then turn out and pierce all over with a fine skewer. Spoon the syrup over the cake, then leave for 20 minutes while it is absorbed. Serve with crème fraîche.

free-form peach pie

Pastry:

225 g plain flour

a good pinch of salt

a good pinch of ground cinnamon

2 tablespoons caster sugar

150 g unsalted butter, straight from
  the fridge, diced

3 tablespoons cold water

Filling:

5 peaches, about 750 g, stoned and
  cut into wedges

3 tablespoons caster sugar, plus extra
  for sprinkling

a large baking tray

serves 4–6

The appeal of this fruit tart is its rustic look.
Use slightly underripe peaches, pears or dessert
apples, depending on what the children prefer.

To make the pastry, briefly pulse the flour, salt, cinnamon
and sugar in a food processor. Add the butter and pulse until
it resembles coarse crumbs. Pour in the water through the feed
tube and process until the dough comes together in a ball.

Gently knead the dough on a lightly floured work surface for a
few seconds until it looks smooth. Roll out the dough to a circle
about 30 cm across on the parchment paper. Chill for 15 minutes.

Preheat the oven to 200°C (400°F) Gas 6. Sprinkle the sliced fruit
with the sugar and mix gently. Remove the dough from the
fridge. Heap the fruit into the centre of the dough evenly. Leave
a wide border of pastry, about 9 cm, without fruit. Gently fold
the border of pastry over the fruit so the fruit in the centre is
uncovered, leaving a gap of about 2 cm between the fruit and the
fold, and gently pinch the pleats of pastry together every 6 cm.
Try not to press the dough down on the fruit.

Brush the pastry with cold water then sprinkle with sugar. Bake
for 40 minutes, until golden. Leave the tart to cool on its tray for
10 minutes then slide off its paper lining. Serve while still warm.

summer fruit tart

80 g plain chocolate, roughly
    chopped

Pastry:
175 g butter, softened
75 g caster sugar
1 egg yolk
250 g plain flour, plus extra to sprinkle

Filling:
250 g mascarpone cheese
2 tablespoons caster sugar
1 kg mixed summer berries (such
    as strawberries, raspberries and
    blueberries)
a 23-cm loose-bottomed tart tin
a pastry brush

serves 6

This tart is bursting with fruity goodness. The
children will love the surprise layer of chocolate
coating the pastry base.

To make the pastry, combine the butter and sugar in a bowl and
beat until smooth. Add the egg yolk and beat again until well
mixed. Stir in the flour and mix until you get a soft but not sticky
dough. Divide the dough in two and freeze half for next time.

Roll out the dough on a lightly floured work surface until it is just
a little bit bigger than the tart tin. Press the pastry gently into the
corners of the tart tin and repair any holes with a little extra
pastry. Trim the edges of the pastry case then pop it in the fridge
for 30 minutes or so, to firm up.

Preheat the oven to 180°C (350°F) Gas 4. Take the tart out of the
fridge and bake for 10–15 minutes until golden. Leave it to cool.

Melt the chocolate in a heatproof bowl set over a saucepan of
simmering water or in the microwave. Leave to cool slightly then
brush the base of the pastry with the chocolate and leave to set.

To make the filling, put the mascarpone and sugar in a bowl and
beat until smooth. Spoon it into the tart case, scatter the berries
evenly over the mascarpone and serve in slices.

seasonal fruit tray tart

500 g puff pastry

1 kg seasonal fruit, such as apples, apricots, nectarines, peaches or plums, cored or stoned, as necessary

1 egg, beaten

50 g unrefined caster sugar

50 g butter

runny honey, for drizzling

icing sugar, for dusting

a baking tray, lightly greased

serves 6

A simple dessert that makes the most of any fruit in season. The children will enjoy getting involved with rolling out the pastry.

Preheat the oven to 180°C (350°F) Gas 4.

Dust a work surface with flour and roll out the pastry to approximately 30 x 30 cm. Lay the pastry out on the prepared baking tray. Arrange the fruit on the pastry in an even layer, leaving a 4-cm border around the edges. Brush the border with the egg and fold inwards all the way around. Sprinkle the fruit with the caster sugar and dot with the butter.

Bake for 45 minutes, reducing the heat if the pastry shows signs of burning. Drizzle with honey and dust with icing sugar before serving. Whipped cream or crème fraîche goes well with this tart.

baked lemon pudding

50 g unsalted butter
285 g caster sugar
3 eggs, separated
3 tablespoons self-raising flour
375 ml whole milk
65 ml freshly squeezed lemon juice
1 tablespoon icing sugar
a medium ovenproof baking dish

serves 6

This custardy lemon dessert will add a zing to the end of any dinner as well as filling the kitchen with lovely citrus aromas. It's cheap to make too.

Preheat the oven to 180°C (350°F) Gas 4.

Put the butter and sugar in a food processor and process for about 10 seconds, until smooth. Add the egg yolks one at a time to the mixture and process for a few seconds after each addition.

Add the flour and process until smooth. With the motor running pour in the milk in a slow and steady stream, scraping down the bowl of the food processer with a spatula so all the mixture is incorporated and lump free. Transfer the mixture to a large bowl.

Using an electric handheld whisk, beat the egg whites until firm, then fold them into the batter in two batches using a large metal spoon. Quickly stir in the lemon juice. Spoon the mixture into the baking dish and bake in the preheated oven for 25–30 minutes, until golden on top.

Let the pudding rest for 10 minutes before dusting with icing sugar to serve.

almond fruit crumble

600 g seasonal fruit such as apples,
  pears, plums, apricots or rhubarb
50 g light brown sugar
125 g self-raising flour
1 teaspoon baking powder
125 g butter, diced
50 g unrefined caster sugar
50 g ground almonds
50 g rolled oats
a 1-litre ovenproof dish, buttered

serves 4

This timeless pudding is always a hit with children and adults alike. The crumble topping keeps well in the fridge so you can always double it up and put some aside for another serving later in the week.

Preheat the oven to 190°C (375°F) Gas 5.

Put the fruit in the prepared dish, add the brown sugar and 100 ml water.

Put the flour, baking powder and butter in a bowl and rub together with your fingertips until the mixture resembles breadcrumbs. Stir in the caster sugar, almonds and oats, then spoon evenly over the fruit. Bake in the oven for 30 minutes. The crumble should be golden and the fruit bubbling up around the edges. Serve with custard, cream or ice cream.

sweet polenta pudding

600 ml whole milk

300 g polenta

120 g caster sugar, plus 2 tablespoons
     for the topping

50 g mixed candied peel

100 g candied orange peel

100 g sultanas

grated zest of 1 large unwaxed orange

50 g salted butter, plus 2 tablespoons
     for the topping

2 eggs

sunflower oil, to grease

single cream, to serve

a baking tray, lightly greased

a biscuit cutter (optional)

a large ovenproof serving dish

serves 4

Children will enjoy this melt-in-the-mouth, comforting pudding. The addition of sultanas and candied peel gives it a great texture.

Pour 600 ml water and the milk into a large saucepan and bring it to the boil over medium heat. Pour the polenta in a steady stream into the pan, stirring quickly with a whisk. Cook the polenta for the time recommended on the packet.

When the polenta is cooked, remove it from the heat. Stir in the sugar, peel, sultanas, grated orange zest and butter until everything is evenly mixed and the butter has melted.

Crack the eggs into a small bowl and beat them until smooth. Stir them into the polenta until everything is well mixed. Pour the mixture out onto the prepared baking tray, then smooth it over with a palette knife. Leave it to cool and set.

When you are ready to cook the polenta, preheat the oven to 200°C (400°F) Gas 6. Cut the polenta into circles using a biscuit cutter or an upside-down glass and lay the circles in the serving dish. To make the topping, melt the remaining butter in a pan. Drizzle the butter and remaining sugar over the polenta circles. Transfer the dish to the preheated oven and bake the polenta for about 15–20 minutes, until golden. Serve with single cream.

brownies & ice cream

4 large eggs

320 g caster sugar

1 teaspoon vanilla extract

140 g unsalted butter, melted

75 g cocoa powder

140 g plain flour

100 g best-quality white chocolate,
broken up into chunks

vanilla ice cream, to serve

*a 20-cm square cake tin, lined with
aluminium foil*

makes 16

Warm fudge sauce:

140 g plain chocolate, roughly
chopped

30 g unsalted butter

2 tablespoons golden syrup

100 ml whole milk or single cream

serves 6

A great mix-and-bake recipe with white chocolate lumps for those who don't or can't eat nuts. For a special birthday meal, serve the brownies warm with ice cream or the warm fudge sauce below.

Preheat the oven to 160°C (325°F) Gas 3.

Crack the eggs into a large mixing bowl. Tip the sugar into the bowl, then add the vanilla. Stir well with a wooden spoon for 1 minute until completely mixed.

Pour in the melted butter and stir for another minute.

Sift the cocoa and flour onto the egg mixture. Stir well for another minute. When there are no streaks of flour left, add the white chocolate chunks. Stir until just mixed, then spoon the mixture into the foil-lined tin.

Bake in the preheated oven for about 40 minutes. Insert a skewer halfway between the sides and the centre – if it is clean, then the brownies are ready, if not, then cook for 5 minutes more. Leave to cool on a wire rack. When completely cold, remove the brownies from the tin then cut into 16 squares. Store in an airtight container and eat within 5 days or freeze for up to 1 month.

To make the warm fudge sauce, put the chocolate, butter, golden syrup and milk or cream in a small saucepan over very low heat. When the butter and chocolate start to melt, stir gently every minute or so to make a smooth sauce. Take off the heat and serve with the brownies. The sauce will keep for a few days in the refrigerator.

baked alaska

500 ml strawberry, raspberry or
    vanilla ice cream
1 ready-made sponge base,
    21 cm in diameter
4 egg whites
230 g caster sugar
150 g raspberries
icing sugar, for sprinkling

makes 1 large cake

Children will love this kitsch dessert that is great fun to make and eat. Use a ready-made sponge or madeira cake for the base to speed up the process and top with your favourite ice cream.

Remove the ice cream from the freezer and leave until soft enough to spoon out. Put the sponge base onto a baking tray, then spoon the ice cream on top to make an even layer. Put the whole thing back into the freezer and leave until very firm – at least 1 hour. It will keep for up to 3 days in the freezer.

When you are ready to finish the alaska, preheat the oven to 220°C (425°F) Gas 7.

Put the egg whites into a very clean mixing bowl. Using an electric mixer or hand whisk, whisk until the whites turn into a stiff white foam – lift out the whisk and there will be a little peak of white standing on the end. Quickly whisk the caster sugar into the egg whites to make a stiff and glossy meringue.

Remove the sponge and ice cream from the freezer. Top with the raspberries. Quickly cover the whole thing with the meringue, making sure there are no gaps. Sprinkle with sifted icing sugar. Bake for just 4–5 minutes, until golden. Serve immediately.

teatime treats

raspberry shortcakes

Base:

200 g plain flour

25 g cornflour

a pinch of salt

75 g caster sugar

150 g unsalted butter, straight
from the fridge, diced,
plus extra for the tin

Filling:

150 g fresh raspberries

125 g good raspberry jam

Topping:

50 g porridge oats

3 tablespoons light brown
muscovado sugar

an 18-cm square cake tin, greased

makes 9 shortcakes

These moreish, buttery shortcakes topped with fresh raspberries are ready in just 30 minutes. Keep some raspberries in the freezer so that you can make the shortcakes year round.

Preheat the oven to 180°C (350°F) Gas 4. Tip the flour, cornflour, salt and sugar into the bowl of a food processor. Pulse for a few seconds to mix the ingredients. Add the butter and work the processor until the mixture looks like fine crumbs.

Weigh out 100 g of the mixture and put to one side for the topping. Tip the rest of the mixture into the prepared tin, making sure it is evenly spread. Bake for 10 minutes then leave to cool while you make the filling and topping. Leave the oven on.

Put the raspberries and jam into a bowl and mix gently. Put to one side. In another bowl, mix together the remaining 100 g shortcake crumbs, the oats and sugar. Squeeze the mixture together with your hands so it comes together into flakes. Spread the raspberry mixture over the baked shortcake then scatter with the oat topping. Bake for another 15–20 minutes, until golden and bubbling around the edges. Leave to cool on a wire rack.

Cut the shortcake into 9 squares. Store in an airtight container and eat within 4 days. It also makes a great dessert with custard.

oaty chocolate crunchies

100 g plain chocolate
    (at least 70 percent cocoa solids),
    roughly chopped
225 g granola
12 paper cupcake cases

makes 12

A little chocolate now and again is fine, all the more so when it's high in iron-rich cocoa solids and melted over nutritious nuts, seeds and oats.

Melt the chocolate in a heatproof bowl set over a saucepan of gently simmering, not boiling, water. Stir it occasionally, until it is smooth. Remove the bowl from the pan.

Add the granola to the chocolate and mix thoroughly. Put about 1 tablespoon of the mixture into each case. Leave for 1 hour until set before serving. Store in an airtight container for up to 1 week.

apricot & walnut flapjack

100 g sunflower margarine
2 tablespoons light muscovado sugar
5 tablespoons golden syrup
200 g porridge oats
75 g ready-to-eat dried apricots,
    chopped
50 g walnuts, chopped
*a baking tin, 18 cm square, lightly
    greased*

makes about 12

These flapjacks are low in fat and packed with fibre, protein and omega-3 fatty acids.

Preheat the oven to 180°C (350°F) Gas 4. Put the margarine, sugar and syrup in a pan and heat gently, stirring occasionally, until the margarine has melted and the sugar has dissolved.

Remove the pan from the heat and add the oats, apricots and walnuts. Stir well until thoroughly mixed, then press into the prepared baking tin with the back of a spoon.

Bake for 20–25 minutes until golden and firm. Leave to cool before cutting into bars. Leave until completely cold before removing from the tin. Store in an airtight container for up to 5 days.

oaty chocolate crunchies

sticky cinnamon buns

Dough:

500 g strong white bread flour

1 x 7-g sachet easy-blend
   (fast action) dried yeast

1 teaspoon salt

3 tablespoons caster sugar

1 large egg,
   at room temperature

300 ml milk, lukewarm

40 g unsalted butter, very soft

Filling:

30 g butter, very soft

1 teaspoon ground cinnamon

4 tablespoons light brown muscovado
   sugar

50 g pecan pieces or raisins

a baking tray, very well greased

makes 12 buns

These buns smell as good as they taste. The recipe yields twelve buns and you'll be hard pressed to keep the children's hands off them.

Put the dry dough ingredients in a bowl and mix. Make a well in the centre. Add the egg, milk and butter in the centre. Use your hands to slowly stir the flour into the liquid in the centre, until it has all been mixed in. If the dough feels dry add a little more milk. If it feels sticky, add a little flour. Gather into a ball and knead for 5 minutes on a floured work surface. Leave the dough covered in a warm place until it has doubled – about 1 hour.

Uncover the bowl and gently punch down the dough. Roll it out on a lightly floured work surface, roll the dough out to a rectangle about 25 x 35 cm. Spread the butter for the filling over the dough. Mix the cinnamon and sugar and sprinkle over the butter. Lastly, scatter the nuts or raisins over the dough and lightly press down.

Roll up the dough from one of the long sides to make a roll, then pinch the 'seam' of the dough to seal it. Cut into 12 pieces. Put the rolls on the baking tray, cut side up so the spiral filling is exposed. Cover the tray with a dry tea towel and leave to rise for 20 minutes. Preheat the oven to 220°C (425°F) Gas 7. Bake the buns for 20 minutes, until golden brown. Eat warm or at room temperature. They will keep for 2 days in a container.

gingerbread teddy bears

115 g butter

2 tablespoons golden syrup

350 g plain flour

1 teaspoon bicarbonate of soda

1 teaspoon ground ginger

175 g soft brown sugar

1 egg, beaten

icing tubes in assorted colours and
    edible balls, to decorate

*teddy bear-shaped biscuit cutters in
    assorted sizes*

2 baking trays, greased

makes about 10 bears

Look out for teddy-bear-shaped biscuit cutters in kitchen shops. Ready-made coloured icing sold in squeezy tubes makes it easier for small children to help with the decorating.

Warm the butter and syrup in a saucepan until melted, then set aside to cool. Combine the flour, bicarbonate of soda, ginger and sugar in a bowl. Make a well in the centre. Pour in the butter and syrup, add the egg, then mix well to combine. Knead lightly to form a soft dough, then wrap it in clingfilm and chill for about 20 minutes.

Preheat the oven to 190°C (375°F) Gas 5.

Roll out the dough on a lightly floured work surface and stamp out the teddy bear shapes using biscuit cutters. Transfer the shapes to the baking trays and bake in the preheated oven for 7–8 minutes, until starting to colour around the edges. Leave to cool on the trays for about 3 minutes, then transfer to a wire rack to cool completely. Decorate the bears as you wish.

peach & almond tarts

110 g wholemeal flour

50 g ground almonds

a pinch of salt

25 g muscovado sugar

100 g polyunsaturated margarine

1 egg, beaten

natural yoghurt, to serve

cubes of fresh peach, to serve

maple syrup or runny honey,
    to serve

a tartlet tray, well greased

makes 8–10 tartlets

Children will love this recipe. Almonds have the highest protein content of any nut as well as being rich in the minerals magnesium, potassium and phosphorous, and especially rich in calcium. They are also high in monounsaturated fat so really, these tartlets are positively good for you!

Preheat the oven to 190°C (375°F) Gas 5.

Mix the flour, almonds, salt and sugar together in a bowl and rub in the margarine. Mix in the egg to form a soft dough.

Roll out the pastry thinly on a lightly floured surface. Cut into 8–10 circles to fit your tartlet tray. Arrange in the tray and bake in the preheated oven for 15 minutes. Leave to cool.

Fill each tartlet with a dollop of yoghurt, then top with the peaches and drizzle with maple syrup.

Store any remaining tartlet cases in an airtight container for up to 2 days, or freeze in batches of 4–6 and warm up in the oven. Try other fillings, such as sliced strawberries mixed with a little elderflower cordial and served with a spoonful of crème fraîche.

white chocolate
& raspberry tartlets

300 g ready-made puff pastry

100 g white chocolate, roughly
   chopped

2 eggs

100 ml double cream,

50 g caster sugar

300 g raspberries

plain flour, to sprinkle

icing sugar, to dust

a 12-hole muffin tin

a biscuit cutter roughly the same size as
   the muffin tin holes

makes 12 tartlets

These little tarts look so elegant and taste great,
yet they're a doddle to make. They will fly off the
plates, straight into your children's sticky mitts.

Preheat the oven to 180°C (350°F) Gas 4.

Turn the dough out onto a lightly floured surface. Using a rolling
pin, roll it out until it is about 2 mm thick. Cut the dough into
rounds using the pastry cutter and press them gently into the
muffin tin holes.

Melt the chocolate in a heatproof bowl set over a saucepan of
gently simmering water, making sure that the bottom of the bowl
does not touch the water. Stir the chocolate with a wooden spoon
until it has melted. Take it off the heat and leave it to cool.

Beat the eggs in a large bowl with a balloon whisk until smooth.
Whisk in the cream and sugar followed by the melted chocolate,
making sure the mixture is nice and smooth.

Carefully fill the tartlet cases with the mixture using a small
spoon. Bake in the preheated oven for about 15 minutes, until the
pastry has puffed up and is golden in colour. Leave to cool. Put
3 or 4 raspberries on top of each tartlet, dust with sifted icing
sugar and serve.

do-it-yourself party cupcakes

115 g unsalted butter,
   at room temperature
115 g caster sugar
2 eggs
115 g self-raising flour
1½ tablespoons cocoa powder

To decorate:
175 g unsalted butter,
   at room temperature
450 g icing sugar, sifted
2 tablespoons milk
lilac, yellow and green food colouring
brightly coloured sweets, such as
   Dolly Mixtures, Smarties and
   Jelly Tots
coloured sprinkles such as hundreds
   and thousands, sugar flowers and
   edible coloured balls
a 12-hole cupcake tin, lined with
   paper cases

makes 12 cupcakes

These decorate-your-own-cakes are always a hit at kids' parties. Everyone will love getting creative and trying to produce the most outlandish cupcake at the table. Just be sure to make plenty of icing and search out lots of pretty decorations.

Preheat the oven to 180°C (350°F) Gas 4.

Beat the butter and sugar in a bowl until pale and fluffy, then beat in the eggs, one at a time. Sift the flour and cocoa powder into the mixture and fold in. Spoon the mixture into the paper cases and bake in the preheated oven for about 17 minutes until risen and a skewer inserted in the centre comes out clean. Transfer to a wire rack to cool completely.

To decorate, beat the butter until soft, then add the sugar and milk and beat until smooth and creamy. Divide the icing among three bowls. Add a few drops of food colouring to each one and stir well to make a vibrant lilac, yellow and green topping. Spoon into serving bowls.

Arrange the cakes on a plate and put the decorations in individual bowls alongside the bowls of icing. Let the children decorate their own cakes.

ice cream cupcakes

60 g unsalted butter,
   at room temperature
60 g caster sugar
1 egg, beaten
60 g self-raising flour

To decorate:
60 g plain chocolate,
   roughly chopped
2½ tablespoons double cream
1 tablespoon golden syrup
ice cream
a 12-hole cupcake tin, lined with
*   paper cases*

makes 12 cupcakes

These cupcakes are perfect for serving at a party but they can be messy so be sure to have plenty of napkins at the ready for wiping sticky fingers! Choose any flavour of ice cream you like.

Preheat the oven to 180°C (350°F) Gas 4.

Beat the butter and sugar in a bowl until pale and fluffy, then gradually beat in the egg. Sift the flour into the mix and fold in. Spoon the mixture into the paper cases and bake in the preheated oven for about 15 minutes until risen and golden and a skewer inserted in the centre comes out clean. Transfer to a wire rack and leave to cool completely. Use a serrated knife to cut a shallow hole out of the centre of the cupcakes. Keep what you've cut out for lids.

To decorate, put the chocolate, cream and syrup in a small saucepan and warm gently, stirring, until the chocolate starts to melt. Remove the pan from the heat and continue stirring until smooth and creamy and the chocolate has melted completely.

Using a melon baller, make small scoops of ice cream and place on top of the cupcakes. Replace the lids of the cakes, then spoon over the chocolate sauce and serve immediately.

chocolate brownie birthday cupcakes

75 g plain chocolate,
  roughly chopped
75 g unsalted butter
1 egg
75 g caster sugar
25 g self-raising flour
50 g shelled macadamia nuts, pecan
  nuts or walnuts, coarsely chopped
2 mini-cupcake tins, lined with petits
  fours cases
12 mini-candles

makes 18 cupcakes

These gooey, chocolatey, nutty baby brownie cakes make a mouth-watering change from the traditional children's birthday cake. Choose any nuts you like – macadamia nuts add a lovely buttery taste. Put the cupcakes on a cake stand or plate and gently press a candle into each one. Turn out the lights, light the candles and voilà!

Preheat the oven to 180°C (350°F) Gas 4.

Put the chocolate and butter in a heatproof bowl set over a pan of gently simmering water. Do not let the bowl touch the water. Stir until almost melted. Remove from the heat and leave to cool for about 5 minutes.

Beat in the egg, then stir in the sugar. Sift the flour into the mixture and fold in, then stir in the nuts.

Spoon the mixture into the petits fours cases and bake in the preheated oven for about 17 minutes until the top has turned pale and crackly and is just firm to the touch. Leave to cool on a wire rack, before serving with a glowing candle in the centre of each cupcake.

fresh fruit torte

Base:

150 g plain flour

1 teaspoon baking powder

½ teaspoon ground cinnamon

50 g caster sugar

yolks from 2 large eggs

50 g unsalted butter, chilled and diced

300 g fresh blueberries, blackberries
or cherries (stoned), OR 400 g
apricots or plums, stoned

Topping:

30 g plain flour

¼ teaspoon ground cinnamon

30 g caster sugar

30 g ground almonds

30 g unsalted butter, chilled and diced

*a springform cake tin about 21.5 cm in
diameter, greased and lined with
greaseproof paper*

makes 1 large torte

Children will almost always favour chocolate over fruit for dessert but this wonderfully rich torte is sure to win them over.

Preheat the oven to 180°C (350°F) Gas 4.

Put the flour, baking powder, cinnamon and sugar into the bowl of a food processor. Pulse to mix the ingredients together. Add the egg yolks and butter to the processor. Pulse to mix all the ingredients until they look like very large crumbs.

Tip the crumbs into the cake tin and spread evenly. Press the mixture firmly into the tin with the back of a spoon to make an even layer. Scatter the blueberries, blackberries or cherries over the cake mixture. If using apricots or plums cut in half, cut each into 8 slices. Arrange the fruit over the base.

Put all the ingredients for the topping into the bowl of the food processor. Process until they look like big breadcrumbs. You can also do this in a bowl using your fingers.

Scatter the topping evenly over the fruit. Put the cake tin on a baking tray then bake for 35 minutes, until golden. Remove from the oven and leave to cool on a wire rack until warm, then unclip the tin and remove the torte. Dust with sifted icing sugar before serving either warm or at room temperature with crème fraîche.

toffee loaf cake

250 g plain flour

1 teaspoon bicarbonate of soda

200 g light muscovado sugar

125 ml plain yoghurt

125 ml milk

1 large egg

20 g unsalted butter, melted

50 g chopped pecan nuts, mixed nuts
   or sultanas

*a 450-g loaf tin, greased and lined
   with greaseproof paper*

makes 1 medium cake

This loaf cake is perfect for picnics and lunchboxes, and you can add the children's favourite nuts or dried fruit to the recipe.

Preheat the oven to 180°C (350°F) Gas 4.

Put the flour, bicarbonate of soda and sugar in a bowl.

Pour the yoghurt into a measuring jug, then top up with the milk to make 250 ml. Break the egg into the jug, add the butter, then mix the ingredients with a fork.

Pour the liquids in the jug into the bowl. Mix well with a wooden spoon for 1 minute, then mix in the nuts or fruit. Spoon the mixture into the tin. Bake in the preheated oven for about 45–50 minutes until golden brown. Insert a skewer into the centre of the cake – if it comes out clean, then the cake is cooked; if it is coated in cake mix, then cook for about 5 minutes more.

Put the tin on a wire rack to cool. Leave for 10 minutes, then lift the loaf out of the tin using the lining paper. Leave until cold on the wire rack. Serve in thick slices. The loaf will keep for up to 4 days in an airtight container or freeze it for up to 1 month.

apple tea bread

280 g wholemeal self-raising flour

125 g light muscovado sugar

1 teaspoon baking powder, sifted

1 teaspoon ground cinnamon

½ teaspoon freshly grated nutmeg

180 g apple, cored and grated

75 g sultanas

50 g walnuts, chopped

100 g unsalted butter, melted

1 egg, beaten

about 80 ml clear apple juice

*a 900-g loaf tin, lightly greased
    and lined with greaseproof paper*

makes 1 loaf

This tea bread is so versatile. It's great eaten just as it is for picnics, but it's also delicious served as a quick snack with some Cheddar cheese and grapes on top. Alternatively, serve it warm topped with a little crème fraîche.

Preheat the oven to 180°C (350°F) Gas 4.

Put the flour, sugar, baking powder and spices in a large bowl and mix. Stir in the grated apple, sultanas and walnuts. Mix well.

Mix in the melted butter, then stir in the beaten egg and the apple juice to give a soft dropping consistency. Add a little more apple juice if the mixture is too stiff.

Spoon the mixture into the prepared tin and bake in the preheated oven for 45–50 minutes until cooked. To check, insert a skewer into the centre of the loaf; it should come out clean. Remove from the oven and leave to cool in the tin. Serve in slices. Store in an airtight container for up to 5 days, or wrap and freeze for up to 1 month.

fresh orange cake

1 unwaxed orange, washed and halved

175 g unsalted butter, very soft, plus extra for greasing the tin

250 g caster sugar

3 large eggs, at room temperature

250 g self-raising flour

1 teaspoon bicarbonate of soda

100 ml milk

3 tablespoons plain yoghurt

3 tablespoons caster or granulated sugar, for the topping

a 900-g loaf tin, greased and lined with greaseproof paper

makes 1 large loaf cake

This all-in-one loaf cake is easy to make so get the children involved. The fresh orange gives it a wonderful flavour.

Preheat the oven to 180°C (350°F) Gas 4.

Remove the pips from one half of the orange, cut it into 8 pieces, skin still on and blend in a food processor until finely chopped. Transfer to a bowl or the bowl of an electric mixer. Add the butter, sugar and eggs then sift in the flour and bicarbonate of soda. Next, add the milk and yoghurt then beat with a spoon or electric mixer (on low speed) for 1 minute until well mixed and there are no streaks of flour. Spoon the mixture into the prepared tin.

Bake for about 50 minutes, until golden. Insert a skewer in the centre of the cake – if it comes out clean, then the loaf is ready. If it is sticky with mixture, then cook the loaf for another 5 minutes.

To make the topping, squeeze the juice of the other orange half into a bowl then stir in the sugar to make a thick, syrupy glaze.

Leave the loaf tin to stand on a wire rack. Prick the top of the loaf all over with a cocktail stick and spoon over the syrup. Leave to cool completely before removing from the tin. Cut the cake into thick slices. Store in an airtight container and eat it within 4 days.

sticky gingerbread

225 g unsalted butter

225 g dark muscovado sugar

225 g black treacle

2 eggs, beaten

340 g plain flour

2 teaspoons ground cinnamon

1 tablespoon ground ginger

1 teaspoon bicarbonate of soda

285 ml warm milk

*2 x 19 x 12-cm loaf tins, greased and
    lined with greaseproof paper*

makes 2 large loaves

This classic teatime recipe yields two loaves – you can bake them both together then pop one in the freezer to eat a week later. Alternatively, if you have a lot of mouths to feed, this cake mix can be baked in one 25-cm round cake tin, but it will need to cook for 1½ hours.

Preheat the oven to 140°C (275°F) gas 1.

Put the butter, sugar and treacle in a large saucepan and heat gently, stirring constantly until melted.

Remove from the heat, leave to cool slightly and then stir in the beaten eggs. Sift the flour, cinnamon and ginger into the melted mixture.

Mix together the bicarbonate of soda and warm milk. Add to the ginger mixture, mix well and pour equal amounts of the cake mix into each tin.

Bake in the preheated oven for just under 1 hour. The top of the cake will be slightly golden with a lovely crust and a skewer should come out clean.

chocolate fudge birthday cake

100 g good plain chocolate,
   roughly chopped

3 tablespoons cocoa powder

100 ml water, very hot but not boiling

175 g unsalted butter, softened

250 g caster sugar

3 large eggs

200 ml plain yoghurt

250 g plain flour

2 teaspoons baking powder

1 teaspoon bicarbonate of soda

Chocolate icing:

100 ml double cream

50 g good milk chocolate,
   roughly chopped

50 g good plain chocolate,
   roughly chopped

your choice of decorations

a springform cake tin, 22.5 cm diameter,
   greased and lined with
   greaseproof paper

serves 8–10

This delicious, chocolatey cake is perfect for birthdays. It tastes best made a day ahead.

Preheat the oven to 160°C (325°F) Gas 3. Put the chocolate, cocoa powder and hot water in a heatproof mixing bowl. Leave for 1 minute then stir until the mix is smooth and melted.

Put the butter and sugar into a bowl. Beat well, then gradually add the eggs and beat until very smooth. Pour in the melted chocolate mixture and mix well. Spoon in the yoghurt, sift in the flour, baking powder and bicarbonate of soda and mix well. Spoon into the prepared tin, then spread evenly so it is smooth.

Bake for 55 minutes. Insert a skewer in the centre of the cake – if it comes out clean, then the cake is ready. If not, bake for another 5 minutes. Remove from the oven and set the tin on a wire rack. Leave to cool for 5 minutes then unclip the tin and leave the cake to cool completely. Don't worry if it sinks a bit.

To make the icing, heat the cream in a pan until it is scalding hot, but not quite boiling. Take off the heat. Put the two kinds of chocolate in a heatproof bowl and pour over the hot cream. Leave for 2 minutes then stir until smooth. Leave to cool.

Put the cake upside down on a plate. Spread the icing on the top and sides of the cake to cover it completely. Decorate with sprinkles and sweets. Leave to cool until firm before serving.

scones

250 g plain flour

4 teaspoons baking powder

a good pinch of salt

50 g caster sugar

50 g unsalted butter, at room
    temperature, diced, plus a
    little extra for greasing

1 large egg, lightly beaten

about 100 ml milk

a baking tray, greased

a biscuit cutter, about 6.5 cm or a
    drinking glass of the same diameter

makes about 8 scones

Scones are quick and easy to make so get the children involved. Add sultanas if you like, or omit the sugar and add some grated cheese.

Preheat the oven to 220°C (425°F) Gas 7.

Sift the flour, baking powder, salt and sugar into a bowl. Rub the butter into the flour with your fingertips until the mixture looks like crumbs. Make a well in the centre.

Put the egg into a measuring jug along with enough milk to make 150 ml in total. Pour three-quarters of the milk mixture into the centre. Using a knife, combine the liquid and flour mix to make a soft, coarse-looking dough. If the dough is dry and crumbly stir in more of the milk mixture a tablespoon at a time.

Work and knead the ball of dough on a lightly floured work surface for a few seconds so it looks smoother. Flatten the dough until it is about 3 cm thick. Dip the cutter in flour then cut out rounds. Gather up the scraps into a ball to make more rounds.

Put all the rounds onto the prepared baking tray, setting them slightly apart and bake in the preheated oven for 12–15 minutes, until golden. Transfer the scones to a wire rack. They taste best eaten the same day.

drinks

lemon cordial

freshly squeezed juice and
grated zest of 6 unwaxed lemons
450 g unrefined granulated sugar

To serve:
lemon slices
ice cubes (optional)

makes 2 litres

Packed with vitamin C, this delicious drink is
sure to quench the children's thirst on a hot day.

Put the lemon juice in a large bowl, add the sugar and stir well.

Put the lemon zest and 1.2 litres cold water in a pan and bring
to the boil. Reduce the heat and simmer for 3 minutes. Strain
through a sieve onto the lemon juice and sugar mixture and stir
until the sugar has dissolved. Discard the zest.

Cover loosely and leave to cool completely. Dilute the cordial
to taste with cold water and add slices of lemon and ice cubes,
if liked. Store in the refrigerator for up to 2 weeks.

apple & carrot juice

3 carrots, chopped
2 eating apples, peeled, cored and
chopped
2 tablespoons crushed ice,
to serve (optional)

serves 2

This juice is high in soluble fibre, which is
necessary for a healthy digestive system, and
is full of immune-boosting antioxidants.

Push the carrot and apple pieces through a juicer. Put
1 tablespoon crushed ice, if using, in each of 2 tall glasses, pour
the juice over the top and serve.

blueberry & orange smoothie

freshly squeezed juice of 4 oranges
1 punnet blueberries (about 250 g)
sugar (optional)

serves 1–2

All fruits contain vitamin C, but oranges contain more than others. Use them to extend fruits that don't have much juice themselves, such as blueberries, strawberries or apricots.

Put the orange juice in a blender, add the blueberries and blend until smooth. Add sugar to taste, if using.

berry, apricot & orange slush

8 ripe apricots, halved and stoned,
  then coarsely chopped
8 strawberries, hulled and halved
freshly squeezed juice of 2 oranges

serves 1

This delightful slush is ready in just minutes and far cheaper to make at home with the children than to buy pre-prepared.

Put the apricots, strawberries and orange juice into a blender and purée until smooth, adding water if needed. (If the mixture is too thick, add ice cubes and blend again.)

fresh raspberry lemonade

2 large unwaxed lemons
75 g caster sugar
175 g fresh or frozen raspberries
500 ml sparkling mineral water
12 ice cubes

serves 4

This fizzy, refreshing, healthy cool drink really is summer in a glass. It's sure to lure the children away from shop-bought carbonated drinks that are laced with additives and sweeteners.

Cut each lemon into 8. Put the lemons, sugar, raspberries and 200 ml cold water in a blender. Blend for 10 seconds. If there are still large pieces of lemon left, blend again for 5 seconds. Remove the blender jug from the machine.

Put a sieve on top of a large serving jug. Carefully pour the lemon mixture into the jug through the sieve. Using a spoon, gently press down on the lemons in the sieve to squeeze out all the juice. Throw away the lemon pieces.

Top up the juice with the sparkling water. Stir in the ice cubes and serve in chilled glasses.

chocolate monkey milkshake

300 ml semi-skimmed milk (use
   whole milk for children under 5)
150 ml natural yoghurt
2 ripe bananas, sliced
2 tablespoons crushed ice (optional)
2 teaspoons finely grated plain
   chocolate (at least 70 percent
   cocoa solids)

serves 2

Bananas are the perfect fast food. They are filling and high in potassium and vitamin B6 – perfect for keeping your little monkeys satisfied.

Put the milk, yoghurt and bananas in a blender and process until smooth. Put 1 tablespoon crushed ice, if using, in each of 2 tall glasses and pour the milkshake over the top. Sprinkle with the grated chocolate and serve immediately.

honey, apple & banana shake

2 ripe bananas, sliced
250 ml natural yoghurt
2 teaspoons runny honey
200 ml clear apple juice
ice cubes, to serve (optional)

serves 2

Try this fruitier twist on the shake above. The honey, apple and banana flavours make a winning combination.

Put the bananas, yoghurt, honey and apple juice in a blender and process until smooth. Pour into 2 tall glasses, add ice cubes, if using, and serve immediately.

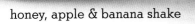
honey, apple & banana shake

mango smoothie

1 ripe mango, peeled and sliced

1 ripe banana, sliced

250 ml chilled fresh orange juice

ice cubes, to serve (optional)

serves 2

Perfect on a really hot day when you want to give your children a filling drink, but would rather avoid a calorie-laden milkshake.

Put all the mango slices and any juice into a large blender or food processor, along with the banana slices. Pour in the orange juice. Blend the mixture until completely smooth and foamy. Pour into tall glasses and add ice cubes, if using.

strawberry milkshake

250 g ripe strawberries, hulled
and sliced

1 ripe banana, sliced

175 ml semi-skimmed milk (use
whole milk for children under 5)

ice cubes, to serve (optional)

serves 2

This is a simple fruit and milk recipe – but you can add a scoop of strawberry ice cream or sorbet if you like.

Put the strawberries and banana into the blender, then add the cold milk. Blend the mixture until smooth and foaming. Pour into chilled glasses and add ice cubes, if using.

peach melba ripple

4 tinned peach halves in natural juice,
    drained
1 teaspoon vanilla extract
500 ml semi-skimmed milk (use
    whole milk for children under 5)
4 scoops vanilla ice cream
125 g raspberries

serves 2–3

You can simply blend all the ingredients for this recipe together in one go, but the children will love the rippled effect of swirling the peach and raspberry flavours together just before serving.

Put the peach halves, half the vanilla extract, half the milk and 2 scoops of vanilla ice cream in a blender. Blend until smooth and divide between 2 or 3 tumblers. Repeat with the raspberries and remaining vanilla, milk and ice cream. Drizzle the raspberry mixture carefully into the glasses to give a ripple effect.

lemon cheesecake shake

100 g cream cheese
grated zest and freshly squeezed juice
    of ½ unwaxed lemon
4 tablespoons lemon curd
125 ml Greek yoghurt
250 ml semi-skimmed milk (use
    whole milk for children under 5)

serves 3–4

Sharp and tangy, this rich drink is just like cheesecake in a glass. Serve it with digestive or ginger biscuits, depending on what the children prefer, and it's almost like having the real thing!

Put all the ingredients in a blender and blend until smooth.

real hot chocolate

real hot chocolate

30 g plain chocolate, roughly chopped

1 teaspoon caster sugar

200 ml semi-skimmed milk (use
   whole milk for children under 5)

To serve (optional):

whipped cream

mini-marshmallows

serves 1

The real thing – plain chocolate, milk and
a dash of sugar, plus whipped cream and mini
marshmallows if you really want to have fun.

Put the chocolate, sugar and milk in a small saucepan. Heat until
almost boiling. Stir occasionally with a wooden spoon to help the
chocolate melt.

Using a whisk, beat the milk until it is very smooth and foaming.
Carefully pour the hot chocolate into a mug. Top with a swirl of
cream, sprinkle with marshmallows, then serve.

vanilla soyaccino

500 ml soya milk

1 teaspoon vanilla extract

4 teaspoons maple syrup

ground cinnamon or powdered
   drinking chocolate, to serve

serves 2

For children who are lactose intolerant, soya milk
is the perfect way of enjoying other 'milky' drinks.

Put the soya milk, vanilla and maple syrup in a saucepan and
gently heat until it just reaches boiling point. Remove from the
heat and then froth the milk, using a milk frother or whisk. Pour it
into 2 cups, dust with ground cinnamon or powdered drinking
chocolate and serve immediately.

babyccino

250 ml semi-skimmed milk (use
    whole milk for children under 5)
2 teaspoons chocolate syrup or sauce
powdered drinking chocolate, to dust
mini-marshmallows, to serve
    (optional)

serves 2

It's always cute to see small children emulating their parents with a 'mini-latte' – of course these are made without coffee but they look great with the drizzle of chocolate syrup.

Put the milk in a saucepan and heat gently until warm, but not hot, then froth the milk using a frother or whisk. Drizzle a little chocolate syrup inside 2 glasses and add the milk. Dust with drinking chocolate, top with marshmallows, if using, and serve.

chocolate milk with ice cream

2 tablespoons powdered drinking
    chocolate
500 ml semi-skimmed milk (use
    whole milk for children under 5)
2 scoops vanilla ice cream
2 tablespoons chocolate syrup
    or sauce

serves 2

This is guaranteed to become a big favourite with the kids. You can top it with any flavour ice cream you like – chocolate or caramel work well.

Combine the drinking chocolate with about 2 tablespoons of the milk and mix to form a smooth paste. Gently heat the remaining milk in a saucepan until it just reaches boiling point and whisk into the chocolate mixture until evenly blended.

Divide between 2 cups and top with a scoop of ice cream and some chocolate syrup. Serve immediately with spoons.

babyccino

index

recipe credits

SUSANNAH BLAKE
Chocolate brownie
  birthday cupcakes
Do-it-yourself
  cupcakes
Gingerbread teddy
  bears
Ice cream cupcakes

**TAMSIN
BURNETT-HALL**
Cornbread muffins
Goan prawn curry
Niçoise tuna
  lunchbox
Tarragon chicken
  casserole

LINDA COLLISTER
American pancakes
  with blueberries
Baked Alaska
Brownies with
  ice cream
Chocolate fudge
  birthday cake
Chorizo & cheese
  muffins
Cornish bread
Free-form peach pie
Fresh fruit torte
Fresh orange cake
Fresh raspberry
  lemonade
Lamb koftas with
  pita pockets
Mango smoothie
Oven-fried chicken
  nuggets with
  potato wedges
Raspberry shortcake
Real hot chocolate
Scones
Sticky cinnamon
  buns
Strawberry milkshake
Sweet & spicy soup
Toffee loaf cake
Tuna pasta salad

Vegetable
  mini-frittatas
Zingy pasta

ROSS DOBSON
Baked lemon
  pudding

SILVANA FRANCO
Charred vegetable
  pizza
Fiorentina pizzas
Pancetta & chicken
  meatballs
Parsley & pancetta
  cannelloni

LIZ FRANKLIN
Creamy pea soup
Leek frittata
Pasta butterflies with
  courgettes, sultanas
  & pine nuts
Salmon skewers
Summer fruit tart
Sweet polenta
  pudding
Upside-down cheese
  & tomato tart
White chocolate &
  raspberry tartlets

TONIA GEORGE
Pappardelle with
  breaded chicken

NICOLA GRAIMES
Carrot & walnut
  muffins

AMANDA GRANT
Apricot slices
Cereal bars
Chicken & red
  pepper stew
Coleslaw
Creamy potato salad
Falafel in pita
Fresh fruit jellies

Lemon shortbread
  with berries
Meaty sandwiches
Potato, pesto &
  tuna salad
Puff pinwheels
Sausage & chutney
  sandwich
Sausage & red
  pepper rolls
Sesame sausages
Smoked mackerel
  pâté
Spinach & onion
  tortilla
Sticky gingerbread

**RACHAEL ANNE
HILL**
Apple & carrot juice
Apple & oat muffins
Apple tea bread
Apricot & walnut
  flapjacks
Beef bourguignon
Berry berry peachy
  purée
Buttermilk drop
  scones with bananas
  & maple syrup
Carrot & hoummous
  pitas
Cheese straws
Chicken & avocado
  rolls
Chilli con carne
Chocolate monkey
  milkshake
Date & seed bars
Easy ratatouille &
  couscous
Fish cakes
Fish pie
Guacamole
Herby trout parcels
Honey, apple &
  banana shake
Hoummous
Iced lollies

Knickerbocker glory
Lemon cordial
Little cherub's cherry
  semolina
Mini-meatballs &
  couscous with
  five-veg sauce
Mozzarella-topped
  herby veg loaf
Muesli
Nut burgers
Oatmeal pots with warm
  strawberry sauce
Oaty chocolate
  crunchies
Pan-fried mini-
  beefcakes with
  sautéed spring
  greens
Peach & almond
  tartlets
Pink porridge
Pumpkin soup
Roasted root dippers
Simple vegetable
  quiche
Smoked salmon
  bagels
Smoked trout &
  farfalle pasta
Sticky toffee &
  apricot sauce
Super-healthy blueberry
  mini-muffins
Wholemeal
  breadsticks with
  avocado & tomato
  dip

**ELSA PETERSEN-
SCHEPELERN**
Alphabet soup
Berry, apricot &
  orange slush
Blueberry & orange
  smoothie

LOUISE PICKFORD
Babyccino

Chocolate milk with
  ice cream
Lemon cheesecake
  shake
Peach melba ripple
Vanilla soyaccino

FRAN WARDE
Almond fruit crumble
Banana, pecan &
  granola yoghurt pot
Chorizo & bean
  pasties
Eggs cocotte
Frozen berry
  yoghurt cup
Lemon polenta cake
Minestrone with

pesto
Omelette
Oven-roasted
  vegetables with
  chickpea & couscous
Pasta with ham &
  peas
Poached eggs
Scrambled eggs
Seasonal fruit tray
  tart
Tomato, basil &
  mozzarella pizza
Wholemeal banana &
  chocolate muffins

photography credits

Key: a=above, b=below, r=right, l=left, c=centre.

CAROLINE ARBER
pages 1, 5, 8r, 10, 17, 18,
21, 36, 79, 86, 98, 117,
167, 172, 176

MARTIN BRIGDALE
pages 193, 198, 201, 202

PETER CASSIDY
page 43

VANESSA DAVIES
pages 9, 29, 33, 34r, 44,
58c, 83, 101, 154c, 180,
206, 218c, 218r, 224,
228, 232

TARA FISHER
pages 2, 3cl, 3cr, 6, 30,
34l, 47, 48, 51, 52, 58l,
60, 67, 68, 71, 76, 80, 85,
89, 90, 93, 94, 96 all, 97,
105, 123, 127, 132, 139,
143, 147, 150, 156, 159,
160, 184r, 194, 212

RICHARD JUNG
page 175

LISA LINDER
pages 34c, 40, 59, 75,
102, 124, 153, 154l, 171,
179, 197

WILLIAM LINGWOOD
pages 109, 110, 118, 121,
218l, 223, 235

NOEL MURPHY
pages 4, 8l, 13, 14, 25,
26, 39, 58r, 63, 64, 114,
131, 136, 144, 154r, 163,
164, 184l, 189, 209, 220,
227

WILLIAM REAVELL
pages 3l, 8c, 22, 56, 106,
113, 140, 149

IAN WALLACE
pages 219, 231

POLLY WREFORD
pages 3r, 35, 55, 72, 128,
135, 155, 168, 183, 184c,
185, 186, 190, 205, 211,
215, 216